Learning Yii Testing

Embrace 360-degree testing on your Yii 2 projects using Codeception

Matteo Pescarin

BIRMINGHAM - MUMBAI

Learning Yii Testing

First published: April 2015

Production reference: 1240415

Published by Packt Publishing Ltd.
Livery Place
35 Livery Street
Birmingham B3 2PB, UK.

ISBN 978-1-78439-227-7

www.packtpub.com

Credits

Author
Matteo Pescarin

Reviewers
Tristan Bendixen
Jesús Peña Cadena
Mark Katkov
Samuel Liew

Commissioning Editor
Akram Hussain

Acquisition Editors
James Jones
Greg Wild

Content Development Editor
Rahul Nair

Technical Editor
Taabish Khan

Copy Editors
Hiral Bhat
Tani Kothari
Vikrant Phadke
Sameen Siddiqui
Trishla Singh
Laxmi Subramanian

Project Coordinator
Suzanne Coutinho

Proofreaders
Stephen Copestake
Safis Editing

Indexer
Hemangini Bari

Production Coordinator
Komal Ramchandani

Cover Work
Komal Ramchandani

About the Author

Matteo Pescarin started his career as a filmsetter. He cofounded a digital agency in 1998 with Emanuele Tozzato and became an expert in Flash in 2001, giving talks and writing guides on it. He later decided to distance himself from closed source technologies and committed himself to open standards and open source, joining the Gentoo Channel Italia, an Italian-wide Linux User Group dedicated to the famous distro. He became passionate about HTML and XML-related semantic technologies, combining, once again, his passion for 2D graphics with programming.

Matteo moved to London, UK, in 2009 after getting a CS degree. While still working on LAMP technologies, he started learning and specializing on the project management and quality assurance side of work, where his major interests still lie.

During his spare time, Matteo pretends to be a world-renowned artist and a formidable cook.

I'd like to thank everyone that in some way or the other supported me. I'd also like to dedicate this book to my father, who helped me the most.

About the Reviewers

Tristan Bendixen is currently studying to get a master's degree in software engineering, having had programming as a passion most of his life. Throughout the years, he has worked as a developer on fairly diverse projects, ranging from commercial and corporate websites, over mobile phone apps, to regular desktop applications.

He continues to work as a software developer during his studies, on paid projects as well as some open source ones that he helps out with when time permits.

Jesús Peña Cadena is a computer systems engineer who has loved computer science since he was a kid. His first experience in software development was in high school where he studied to be a computer technician. He fell in love with software so much so that he decided to study his major in Universidad de la Sierra, which is located in Moctezuma, Sonora, where he obtained the keys to grow himself and became a proactive IT professional in the area of software development.

Over the last few years, he has been developing web applications, most of the time working with PHP in the backend and with technologies such as HTML5, JavaScript, and CSS in the frontend. His first job as an engineer was in eDesarrollos (`http://edesarrollos.com`), where he learned a lot more about the software development process.

When he's not tinkering with code, he could be learning something new or spending quality time with his girlfriend, Valeria, his family, and friends.

Many thanks to God for giving me the ability to live and learn in this amazing world. I am also grateful to the Yii framework community because it helped me to become interested in this beautiful framework. In the end, I want to thank my parents for always helping me with their best effort (Philippians 4:13 and Psalm 23:4).

Mark Katkov (https://github.com/Ragazzo) started developing for web in 2008 while working on a VoIP project. There, he introduced the first version of the Yii framework and used Codeception, Behat, and Mink for testing purposes, learning a lot about the tools and testing in general.

Since then, he has handled various projects from simple blog engines to complex enterprise systems, mastering his skills using both Yii 1 and Yii 2.

Currently, Mark is busy with enterprise e-commerce projects in the travel industry, which are developed and maintained according to TDD and DDD.

Apart from commercial jobs, he has contributed significantly to several open source projects, such as the Yii framework, Codeception, and Faker. Currently, he is helping the Yii team with everything that is TDD related.

I would like to thank Matteo Pescarin for sharing his great TDD knowledge, which is vital for Yii developers to make their projects better. This book contains a lot of useful information that can help beginners to not only find their starting point towards learning what TDD is and how it can help them, but also to master the TDD approach.

I would also like to thank Alexander Makarov (https://github.com/samdark), a Yii core team member, for helping us figure out which topics are especially interesting for people developing with the Yii framework.

Finally, thanks to Michael Bodnarchuk (https://github.com/DavertMik), creator of Codeception, for explaining how Codeception works internally and helping me out in difficult situations.

Samuel Liew lives in Singapore and is a full-stack web developer who enjoys producing solutions with interesting and challenging requirements. He has been involved with creating two proprietary content management systems using C#.NET/MongoDB and PHP/Yii/MySQL. His latest accomplishment is developing a microstock photography website (`http://vivistock.com/`) using the Yii Framework, which involves e-commerce transactions and implements heavy business logic.

www.PacktPub.com

Support files, eBooks, discount offers, and more

For support files and downloads related to your book, please visit www.PacktPub.com.

Did you know that Packt offers eBook versions of every book published, with PDF and ePub files available? You can upgrade to the eBook version at www.PacktPub.com and as a print book customer, you are entitled to a discount on the eBook copy. Get in touch with us at service@packtpub.com for more details.

At www.PacktPub.com, you can also read a collection of free technical articles, sign up for a range of free newsletters and receive exclusive discounts and offers on Packt books and eBooks.

https://www2.packtpub.com/books/subscription/packtlib

Do you need instant solutions to your IT questions? PacktLib is Packt's online digital book library. Here, you can search, access, and read Packt's entire library of books.

Why subscribe?

- Fully searchable across every book published by Packt
- Copy and paste, print, and bookmark content
- On demand and accessible via a web browser

Free access for Packt account holders

If you have an account with Packt at www.PacktPub.com, you can use this to access PacktLib today and view 9 entirely free books. Simply use your login credentials for immediate access.

Table of Contents

Preface   **v**

Chapter 1: The Testing Mindset   **1**

Understanding the importance of testing   **2**

Involving project management   **4**

  Estimating tasks   5

  Testing approaches   6

    Introducing Test Driven Development   9

  Planning tests   11

  Generating tests   11

Obtaining the testing mindset   **12**

  Starting with no testing culture – a practical approach   13

Summary   **15**

Chapter 2: Tooling up for Testing   **17**

Downloading and installing Yii 2   **17**

Environment and workflow   **18**

Introducing Composer   **20**

  Installing and using it   20

    The composer.json and composer.lock files   22

    Packages and Packagist   24

  Creating your first web app   27

  The CLI command line   29

Finding your way around Yii 2   **30**

Structure of the default web application   **32**

  Documentation and sample code   33

Defining our working strategy   **33**

  Key features to be implemented   33

    User authentication REST interface   35

    User login from a modal window   35

Introducing testing for our purposes   **35**
  Using a top-down approach versus a
  bottom-up approach   40
  What to test and what not to test   41
  The master test plan   42
Summary   **43**

Chapter 3: Entering Codeception   **45**
Getting started with Codeception   **46**
  A modular framework rather than just another tool   47
  Outlining concepts behind Codeception   47
  Types of tests   48
    AcceptanceTester   49
    FunctionalTester   51
    UnitTester   53
  Other features provided by Codeception   54
Installing Codeception in Yii 2   **56**
  Finding your way around Codeception   57
  Configuring Codeception   58
  Tests available in Yii 2   60
Interacting with Codeception   **61**
  Creating tests   62
  Migrations on the test database   62
Summary   **63**

Chapter 4: Isolated Component Testing with PHPUnit   **65**
Understanding the work to be done   **65**
Using the User model   **66**
Implementing the first unit test   **67**
  How much to care for other people's code   69
Component testing of the model   **70**
  What's testing for PHPUnit   72
  Testing the methods inherited by IdentityInterface   73
  Using data providers for more flexibility   75
  Using fixtures to prepare the database   77
  Adding the remaining tests   80
Implementing the ActiveRecord class and its methods   **80**
  Dealing with migrations   80
  The Gii code generation tool   83
Seeing tests pass   **87**
  Using global fixtures   88
Summary   **90**

Chapter 5: Summoning the Test Doubles   91
Dealing with external dependencies   91
Isolating components with stubs   93
Listening for calls with an observer   96
   Introducing mocking   97
     Getting to know the Yii virtual attributes   98
Writing maintainable unit tests   102
   Using BDD specification testing   103
Summary   105

Chapter 6: Testing the API – PHPBrowser to the Rescue   107
Functional tests in Yii 2   107
   Understanding and improving the available CEPTs   108
   Writing reusable page interactions   112
   Implementing fixtures   113
   Pitfalls of functional tests   116
Functional tests for REST interfaces   116
   Defining the API endpoints   118
   Implementing the tests for the API   119
Creating a RESTful web service with Yii 2   121
   Writing modular code in Yii   121
   Creating a module with Gii   122
   Using modules in Yii 2   124
   Converting our controller to be a REST controller   124
   Adding the access check and security layer   126
     Building the authentication layer   128
   Modifying the existing actions   130
   Adding a new endpoint with parameters   131
Summary   133

Chapter 7: Having Fun Doing Browser Testing   135
Introducing Selenium WebDriver   136
   Installing and running Selenium Server   137
     Configuring Yii to work with Selenium   137
   Implementing WebDriver-led tests   138
Creating acceptance tests   141
   Implementing the modal window   142
   Making the server side work   144
   Adding the JavaScript interaction   144
   Tying everything together   148
     Dealing with Yii 2 assets bundles   148
   Finalizing the tests   150

Testing multiple browsers 152
Understanding Selenium limits 154
Summary **154**
Chapter 8: Analyzing Testing Information **155**
Improving the quality of your tests **155**
Enabling code coverage in Codeception 157
Extracting the code coverage information for unit tests 158
Generating a detailed coverage report of the unit tests 160
Aggregating functional tests to unit tests 164
Generating acceptance tests' coverage report 166
Improving our code with the aid of additional tools **169**
Summary **171**
Chapter 9: Eliminating Stress with the Help of Automation **173**
Automating the build process **174**
Introducing continuous integration systems 174
Available systems 175
Installing and configuring Jenkins 176
Understanding the Jenkins organization 176
Installing the required plugins 180
Creating the required build files **181**
Understanding the basic Ant structure 181
Adjusting the build.xml file 182
Preparing the environment for the build 185
Adding the required configuration settings 187
Adding Composer, Yii, and Codeception support in Ant 188
Configuring the Jenkins build **190**
Generic build settings 191
Build settings 191
Postbuild settings 191
Executing the job 192
Going forward **193**
Summary **194**
Index **195**

Preface

Since I've stumbled upon Yii first and Codeception later on, I couldn't believe that someone actually thought of solving the eternal damnation of a difficult testing panorama that most web developers, including me, have suffered with for so many years.

I've poured a good part of myself into this book, hoping that I could finally create a book that I never managed to find when I needed to learn about testing.

I believe the hardest part has been concentrating all of the accumulated experience, reading, conferences, and chats I've had about quality assurance, testing, and project management.

But this wouldn't have been possible without the great effort that has been put into Yii in its current version (version 2) and Codeception. Both these pieces of software, and the rest that are noted throughout the book, are the result of the efforts of hundreds of developers across the globe.

With all of this, together with the compassion and patience of Cristina, who tolerated my restless evenings to exhaustion, I have the pleasure to release this book, hoping that you will find an inspiration to discuss, improve, and contribute to the testing and web development community.

What this book covers

Chapter 1, *The Testing Mindset*, starts by defining the concepts used throughout the book, tries to explain why testing is so important, introduces the major testing techniques, and shows you how to get into the right mindset to approach this book.

Chapter 2, *Tooling up for Testing*, introduces Yii 2 with an overview for you to understand how the code is organized. We also start defining the work that will be carried over to the remaining chapters from the testing perspective.

Chapter 3, *Entering Codeception*, introduces Codeception and explains what it does, how it's structured, and how it works.

Chapter 4, *Isolated Component Testing with PHPUnit*, demonstrates PHPUnit. The first unit tests are implemented in this chapter, with the help of data providers.

Chapter 5, *Summoning the Test Doubles*, introduces test doubles with the use of mocks and stubs, while still sticking to PHPUnit. We also appreciate an alternative BDD-like syntax to write our tests.

Chapter 6, *Testing the API – PHPBrowser to the Rescue*, gives an overview of functional tests and then shows their expansion relative to the REST interface that Yii 2 allows you to create.

Chapter 7, *Having Fun Doing Browser Testing*, finally shows some live action with acceptance tests using Selenium WebDriver.

Chapter 8, *Analyzing Testing Information*, covers some more advanced topics about tests and code optimization techniques, thanks to the reports generated by Codeception and other tools.

Chapter 9, *Eliminating Stress with the Help of Automation*, is a more advanced chapter and introduces continuous integration with the aim of automating tests and displaying their reports using Jenkins CI.

What you need for this book

This book requires very little to start with. If you've got a decent development machine, the only other thing that you need to install and set up for yourself is a LAMP stack.

If you've worked in this field previously, you might be already aware that there are many other variants that allow you to use a perfectly compatible LAMP stack, such as Nginx, PostgreSQL, or something else. You can even run everything in a VPS or a virtual machine sitting on your local hard drive. This book does not come with instructions on how to set up everything as you need, so be prepared to get something up and running before opening the browser.

Who this book is for

Given the required understanding of the underlying software and service layer, this book can be approached by anyone with some experience in web development and knowledge of OOPHP programming. A seasoned programmer should have no problems approaching this book, as it can be considered a way of increasing and reaffirming their knowledge in testing techniques and practices.

Even though it will be beneficial to have knowledge of testing, it's not strictly required because every aspect of it will be covered, from the theoretical side to the deeply practical side.

Conventions

In this book, you will find a number of text styles that distinguish between different kinds of information. Here are some examples of these styles and an explanation of their meaning.

Code words in text, database table names, folder names, filenames, file extensions, pathnames, dummy URLs, user input, and Twitter handles are shown as follows: "Remember, there's always a README.md file you can consult."

A block of code is set as follows:

```
if (YII_ENV_DEV) {
    // configuration adjustments for 'dev' environment
    $config['bootstrap'][] = 'debug';
    $config['modules']['debug'] = 'yii\debug\Module';
```

When we wish to draw your attention to a particular part of a code block, the relevant lines or items are set in bold:

```
// tests/codeception.yml
...
config:
    test_entry_url: https://basic.yii2.sandbox/index-test.php
```

Any command-line input or output is written as follows:

```
$ cd tests/codeception
```

New terms and **important words** are shown in bold. Words that you see on the screen, for example, in menus or dialog boxes, appear in the text like this: "Just remember to tick the **Overwrite** checkbox and click on **Generate**."

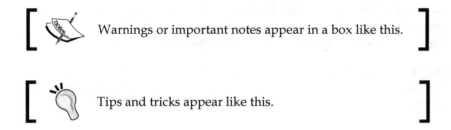

> Warnings or important notes appear in a box like this.

> Tips and tricks appear like this.

Reader feedback

Feedback from our readers is always welcome. Let us know what you think about this book—what you liked or disliked. Reader feedback is important for us as it helps us develop titles that you will really get the most out of.

To send us general feedback, simply e-mail feedback@packtpub.com, and mention the book's title in the subject of your message.

If there is a topic that you have expertise in and you are interested in either writing or contributing to a book, see our author guide at www.packtpub.com/authors.

Customer support

Now that you are the proud owner of a Packt book, we have a number of things to help you to get the most from your purchase.

Downloading the example code

You can download the example code files from your account at http://www. packtpub.com for all the Packt Publishing books you have purchased. If you purchased this book elsewhere, you can visit http://www.packtpub.com/support and register to have the files e-mailed directly to you.

Errata

Although we have taken every care to ensure the accuracy of our content, mistakes do happen. If you find a mistake in one of our books—maybe a mistake in the text or the code—we would be grateful if you could report this to us. By doing so, you can save other readers from frustration and help us improve subsequent versions of this book. If you find any errata, please report them by visiting http://www.packtpub.com/submit-errata, selecting your book, clicking on the **Errata Submission Form** link, and entering the details of your errata. Once your errata are verified, your submission will be accepted and the errata will be uploaded to our website or added to any list of existing errata under the Errata section of that title.

To view the previously submitted errata, go to https://www.packtpub.com/books/content/support and enter the name of the book in the search field. The required information will appear under the **Errata** section.

Piracy

Piracy of copyrighted material on the Internet is an ongoing problem across all media. At Packt, we take the protection of our copyright and licenses very seriously. If you come across any illegal copies of our works in any form on the Internet, please provide us with the location address or website name immediately so that we can pursue a remedy.

Please contact us at copyright@packtpub.com with a link to the suspected pirated material.

We appreciate your help in protecting our authors and our ability to bring you valuable content.

Questions

If you have a problem with any aspect of this book, you can contact us at questions@packtpub.com, and we will do our best to address the problem.

1
The Testing Mindset

This book has been written with the intention of teaching how to use **Codeception** in conjunction with **Yii 2**. By using these two great frameworks, I confirmed that testing could finally become something that anyone would appreciate doing, rather than considering it an odd and not particularly clear appendix of development.

For this reason, this first chapter tries to address several aspects that are rarely touched on but hopefully should give you the understanding and required push to learn and adopt testing, and, on a larger scale, promote testing as a way to improve development as a methodology.

In this chapter, you will see the reason for testing and why testing should be planned into a project, and not done as an afterthought.

You will also see what will happen when you start testing: the implicit and explicit benefits for the short and long term, such as a change of mentality toward testing, the ability to improve component specifications, and architectural, design, and implementation choices, as well as refactoring, redistribution, and overall quality of code.

In order to explain why testing is so important, I'll also briefly dive into the organizational part of the process where **Test Driven Development** (TDD) and **Behavior Driven Development** (BDD) will be explained in relation to modern project management techniques, such as Agile and XP in a multi-skilled, self-organized team.

You will also see how the whole team environment can be improved and re-organized to help share knowledge and speed up workflow.

This chapter has been divided into the following three sections:

- Understanding the importance of testing
- Involving project management
- Obtaining the testing mindset

Understanding the importance of testing

Since I started getting into quality assurance and testing in a professional way, I've never faced myself with the question of "what is testing?"

I have to be honest, but during my time at university, testing wasn't part of any course. I don't really know if this has changed recently, nor if what's being taught is of any importance or relevance to the business world.

In this book, I've tried to combine the practicality of development and testing using a great PHP framework, Yii at its version 2, and the testing suite of Codeception. I will present each topic with a keen eye on the actual benefit for the team, while showing from a higher perspective the planning and the organization of the work. Throughout the chapters in this book, I'll shift back and forth, trying to give a clear understanding of the details you will be working on and the scope of the work, the overall aim from a testing perspective.

But, before we venture into this journey, what effectively is testing? Google engineering director James Whittaker's words make a very good answer to that:

> *"Although it is true that quality cannot be tested in, it is equally evident that without testing, it is impossible to develop anything of quality."*

There are aspects of testing that are so completely fused with development that the two end up being practically indistinguishable from each other, and at other times it is so independent that developers are not even aware that this is happening.

In the whole project lifespan, you start with ideas and transform them into features or stories, breaking them down into tasks. From there you move into the execution of each of these tasks that will hopefully grant you, at the end of them all, a finished product.

At any point in our development process, we have tried to put some level of quality in it, either by "checking" the page loaded or by doing some more smart and deep, if not automated, testing.

Atlassian's QA team lead Penny Wyatt points out that teams where quality assurance was not performed or left alone to perform small automation tasks, with unit tests for instance, had the highest story rejection rate, which is when a story will have to be re-opened after being completed because of wrong or missing functionality. We are talking about a 100 percent of rejection rate.

When such a situation occurs, we are left in a state where we have to go back into development and fix what we've done. This is not the only case: together with it, late discovered bugs and defects, and fixing them, are possibly some of the most expensive tasks in software development. In most cases, it has been shown that their cost is also way higher than it would have been to prevent them in the first place. Unfortunately, software development is rarely devoid of defects, and this should always be kept in mind.

As developers and managers, one of the goals we should have is to reduce the occurrence of defects to an economically acceptable level, and doing this also reduces the resulting risk associated with it.

As a practical example, a large website might have thousands of software errors but still be economically viable due to the fact that 99 percent of the website is displayed correctly. For a Falcon rocket or a Formula 1 car, a defect rate that high is not acceptable: the risk of having a single one in the wrong place might also cost the lives of people.

The other implicit aim for defect reduction is an investment in teamwork. An error introduced by one developer can have a ripple effect on the work of other team members and, overall, trust in the code base and other colleagues' work. In this chapter, and the later chapters, we are going to discuss this aspect in more detail by introducing some concepts of project management and how it can cooperate in ensuring that quality is ensured on many levels.

The last and possibly an equally important aspect is how testing can be used to document the code by example. This is rarely discussed or brought to the attention of developers, but we will see how tests can describe the functionality of our implementations in a way more precise manner than what PHP documentation comments can provide. I'm not saying documentation comments are useless, quite the contrary: in modern **integrated development environments** (IDE) such as NetBeans or PHPStorm, auto-completion and code hinting are a great way to improve the time to discover the underlying framework without having the need to search through a reference manual. Tests can and should in fact provide the much needed help a developer might need when trying to combine and use yet unknown interfaces.

When working with open source software that is a result of the work of a small self-organized team, having the ability to provide documentation without an extensive effort might be the key to rapid and continuous delivery.

But how do we ensure a delivery can be met within constraints that are imposed on the team? In order to explain this, we will have to take a quick detour into project management, from where some of the practices that are discussed and used in this book have been originating.

Involving project management

If you ever have been involved in the planning phase of software development, or if you've worked as a project manager, you should have well in mind that there are three basic variables that you can leverage upon in order to manage projects:

- Time
- Quality
- Cost

In most of the business scenarios described theoretically and practically, the stakeholders decide to fix two of these variables, leaving the team to estimate the third. In other words:

> *Time, Quality and Cost... pick two.*

In reality, what normally happens is that time and cost end up being set outside the project, thus leaving quality as the only variable developers can play on.

You might have already experienced that lowering quality doesn't eliminate work, it will just postpone it. Bringing back what we said earlier regarding defect rates, reducing quality might actually end up increasing the costs in the long run, leaving technical debt to spiral out of control if not causing a lot of problems in the short term.

 The term **technical debt** has been introduced as a metaphor referring to the consequences of bad design, or architectural or development choices in a codebase. A number of books have been written specifically to counterbalance bad practices that are not naturally aimed at managing it.

One of the agile methodologies that are nowadays not particularly talked about, **Extreme Programming (XP)**, has introduced, if not rather exposed, a new variable into the equation: **scope**.

By making scope explicit, it does the following:

- Creates a safe way to adapt
- Provides a way to negotiate
- Gives us a tool to keep requests and demands under control

From the XP point of view, after the breakdown phase, we will have to go through a phase of estimating each single task, and based on the budget, you just keep adding or removing tasks.

This discussion brings up a problem that is currently widely discussed in the community, as estimating tasks is not as easy one might think. We'll dive into it shortly, as I've seen too many misunderstandings of this topic.

Estimating tasks

As we've seen, estimation of the tasks has always been considered one of the fundamental principles of how the delivery path of a project is scheduled. This is especially valid in agile methodologies, as they use fixed time iterations and compute the amount of features and tasks that can be fitted in the given sprint and adjusted at each iteration using tools such as the burn down chart.

 If you've worked in agile environments, this should be pretty much easy to understand, and if you haven't, then there's plenty of information that can be gained by reading books or articles on SCRUM that are freely available online.

Unfortunately, with all the importance estimation has, it seems like nobody really looked deeper into it: there are plenty of articles that warn how much software development task estimations are always off by a factor of 2 or 3. So, should we just swallow the fact that we won't get better at estimating or is there something more to it?

The "estimations do not work" argument is probably not correct either, and recently the hashtag #NoEstimates has sparked a bit of discussion online, which is probably worth including here.

As a matter of fact, estimations do work. The only detail that is normally overlooked is that the estimation is nearing the actual time spent on it depending on how much knowledge the developer has and how much controllable the environment is.

In fact, the reality is twofold: from one side, we will get better at estimating the greater our experience is, and, on the other side, our estimation will be closer to reality if there are less unknowns in our path.

This is well-known in project management as the *Cone of Uncertainty*.

What we really need to do is admit and expose all the aspects that would increase the risk and the uncertainty of our estimations, while trying to isolate what we know is going to take a specific amount of time.

As an example, having a fixed time investigation period to create working prototypes of the features we are going to implement sets a precedent for future computations, while human factors will need to be factored in.

While estimations are particularly important from the business perspective of software development and project management, we won't be touching them again in this book. I'd rather focus on more practical aspects of the development work flow.

Testing approaches

Extreme Programming tries to stress the investment in defect reduction.
In order to do so, it introduces two basic principles: **double-checking** and **Defect Cost Increase (DCI)**.

Double-checking *is* software testing. We know how a particular feature should be working, which can be represented through a test. When implementing such a feature, we know in a quasi-deterministic way that what we've done is actually correct.

Extreme Programming makes use of values, principles, and practices to outline the core structure of the methodology: in short, you pick values that describe you as a team; you adhere to certain principles that will lead you into using specific practices.

Principles can be considered the bridge between values and practices, justifying the use of practices on something more concrete than a mere "but everybody's using it."

The other principle of **DCI** can be used to increase the cost-effectiveness of testing. What DCI states is the following:

> "*The sooner you find a defect, the cheaper it is to fix.*"
>
> *Kent Beck*

To make this even more clearer with an example, if you find a defect after years of development, it could take a lot of time to investigate both what the code was originally meant to be doing and what was the context it was developed in the first place. If, instead, you find the defect the minute it's being implemented, the cost to fix it will be minimal. This, clearly, doesn't even take into consideration all the hidden costs and risks that a severe bug can cause to critical sections of our code base; think about security and privacy for instance.

Not only the longer we wait the more difficult the defects will be to be amended, but also their cost will increase and have the potential to leave many residual defects.

This means that by adhering to DCI, firstly, we need to have shorter feedback cycles so that we can continuously find as many defects as possible, and, secondly, we will have to adopt different practices that can help us keep the cost and the quality untouched as much as we can.

The idea of finding defects rapidly and often has been formalized as **Continuous Integration (CI)** and requires bringing automated testing into play to avoid the costs spiraling out of control. This practice has gained a lot of momentum outside XP and it's currently used widely in many organizations regardless of the project management methodology adopted. We will see how CI and automation can be introduced in our work flow and development in more detail in *Chapter 9, Eliminating Stress with the Help of Automation*.

These practices defy entirely the idea of working in a waterfall way, as shown in the following figure:

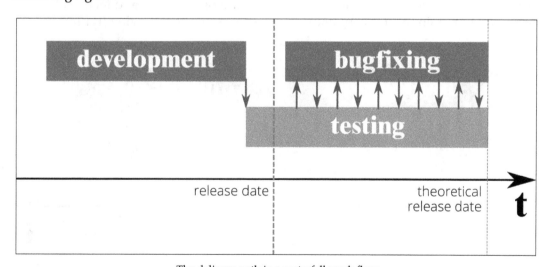

The delivery path in a waterfall work flow

In waterfall, we have a combination of factors that could impact the quality of the work we're doing: in most of the situations where this was the norm, the specifications are not set at the beginning nor frozen at any time. This means that it's very likely we might not produce what the business is asking.

In other words, you would begin testing only after development, which is way too late, as you can see from the preceding figure: you will be unable to actually catch any of the defects in time for the release date. Unfortunately, as much as waterfall might feel natural, its effectiveness has been disproved multiple times and I won't invest more time on this topic.

[

It's worth mentioning that the definition of "waterfall", although without using this term specifically, was formalized by Winston W. Royce in 1970, when describing a flawed and non-working model for software management.
]

Since the advent of agile methodologies, which XP is part of, there has been a great effort to bring testing as early as possible.

Remember that testing is as important as development, so it should be quite clear that we need to treat it as a first-class citizen.

One of the common situations you might find yourself in is that even if you start testing right at the beginning while the code base is being developed, it could potentially raise more issues than those that are needed or can be addressed. The resulting situation will still generate a good amount of problems and technical debt that won't fit within the delivery path, as you can see in the following figure:

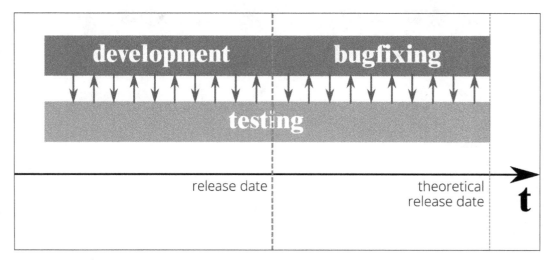

The delivery path in an agile environment

The team's goal is to eliminate all post-development testing and shift testing resources to the beginning. If you have forms of testing such as stress or load testing that highlight defects at the end of the development, try to bring them into the development cycle. Try to run these tests continuously and automatically.

Transitioning into a work flow that has testing at the beginning brings to the surface two main problems: the accumulation of technical debt and the inherent problem that developers and testers are considered two separate entities. Don't forget that there will be still some testing that will happen after development and will clearly need to be performed by third parties, but, nonetheless, let's stress the fact that our efforts are to reduce it as much as we can.

As I'll constantly remind you, testing is not someone else's problem. Instead, with this book I'm aiming at giving the developers all the tools that can make him/her a tester first. There are different approaches to this problem, and we'll address them shortly at the end of this chapter, when talking about the testing mentality.

Introducing Test Driven Development

If you have ever developed with tests in mind, you might have appreciated that getting it right from the beginning is crucial. So, what do we need to test?

Throughout the years, various methodologies have been created that provide a set of rules for the developer that address how to include testing in the development cycle.

The first and most well-known is **Test Driven Development**.

The main objective of adopting TDD as a practice in your team is to achieve the test-first mentality, and this is done using the concept of Red-Green-Refactor. You implement the tests first, which shouldn't pass (red status), you implement the interface being tested allowing the tests to pass (green status), and then you refactor the interface to improve what the test has highlighted, if needed.

We've seen the benefits from the management point of view of using this approach, but there's a more direct impact on the developer side. TDD in fact allows you to achieve what is being taught in software development, that interfaces shouldn't be influenced by the implementations. And, as a secondary effect, it provides, as we've seen, a way to document the interface itself.

By implementing tests first, you focus on how the method, class, and interface should be used by anyone inside or outside your team. This is called **black box testing**, which means that our tests should be completely unaware of the implementation details. This brings the implicit benefit of allowing the implementation to change over time.

If you're interested in this topic, you might find worth exploring the **Design by Contract** (**DbC**) specification that allows you to describe interfaces in a more formal way in specific object-oriented programming languages. A good starting point might be found at `http://c2.com/cgi/wiki?DesignByContract`.

Unfortunately, TDD tries to focus on the atomic part of the features being developed, and it fails to give a broader vision of everything, of what has been tested and how much, or, even better, if what has been tested is of any relevance for the business and the product itself.

Once again, XP, in order to gain the full benefits of double-checking, introduces the following two sets of tests:

- One set written from the perspective of the programmers
- Another set written from the perspective of the users

In the first case, it allows the programmers to test all the system's components exhaustively, and in the latter case, the operation of the system as a whole.

The latter can in a way be seen as what **Behavior Driven Development** (**BDD**) describes in a more formal way. We're going to cover BDD in more detail in *Chapter 2*, *Tooling up for Testing*.

BDD tries to cover TDD's lack of overall scope and shifts the attention to the behavioral aspect of the project. BDD is effectively an evolution of TDD but requires some changes in the organization of the work and the way it's shipped, which can be quite difficult to introduce in some environments without re-assessing the whole workflow.

With BDD, you define what to test and how to test it on multiple levels, detailing the scope of testing using a well-defined, business-oriented language called **ubiquitous language**, borrowed by **Domain-driven Design** (**DDD**) that is shared among all members of the team, both technical and non-technical. For the scope of this chapter, it should suffice to say that BDD introduces the concept of stories and scenarios giving the developer the ability to formally describe the user perspective and functionality of your application. Tests should be written using the standard agile framework of a user story: "As a [role] I want [feature] so that [benefit]." Acceptance criteria should be written in terms of scenarios and implemented as classes: "Given [initial context], when [event occurs], then [ensure some outcomes]."

Planning tests

Planning is, hence, critical when stepping into testing from a software development point of view, and in not-so-recent years, there have been several solutions to improve testing from a planning perspective that give a more detailed and compact way to define the so-called test plan.

In a testing-oriented environment, test plans should give you the direction and the indications of what and how much to test at any level. Moreover, the test plan is something that should be exposed to the various stakeholders and its visibility shouldn't live within the walls of development. Due to this, it's our responsibility to maintain and let this document live throughout the life of the project.

In practice, I've seen this rarely happening because test plans are never formalized or, if they are, they are too long and hard to maintain, suffering from a very short lifespan since their initial conception.

As an example, **Attributes-Components-Capabilities (ACC)** has been created by Google in order to solve some of the main problems that test plans have always suffered, especially their maintainability. You can find more information about ACC and Google Test Analytics software at `https://code.google.com/p/test-analytics/`.

ACC test plans are short and compact, and the whole project tries to aim to test plans that could be created in minutes and that are self-describing and valuable to anyone close to the project.

For each component, you have a series of capabilities, which can be described with one or more attributes; think, for instance, "secure", "fast", or "user-friendly". On top of this, each capability and component has a relative risk level associated with it. These two things together allow you to understand what is most important to test and how thorough your testing should be.

Generating tests

Clearly, planning tests is just the beginning. Once you get into the implementation side, you can pick up this book, which provides the knowledge of how to use the tools available to create tests.

There isn't much more I can tell you about this aspect. You probably just need to read it all, but it should be stressed that there are some basic principles you must keep in mind when writing tests.

Good tests exhibit the following three important characteristics:

- **Repeatability**: Tests must be deterministic. This ensures tests aren't dependent on external factors issues.

- **Simplicity**: Test only one thing. The smaller the test the more controllable it is.

- **Independence**: Tests should execute in isolation. There should be no dependency between tests. This also improves debugging of both the tests and your code.

Once you've got a grip of how to approach a project, viewing it from the architectural point of view, and once you've understood how test plans work and what you really need to test, you can start implementing tests, discuss them, and improve the tools and the way you're using them with the help of your colleagues.

Obtaining the testing mindset

So, up until now, we've seen how important testing is in current development practices and we've seen all kind of aspects that revolve around development itself from a project managing point of view, but still we don't know what's needed to become a good tester.

Finding developers knowledgeable about testing is particularly difficult, and there are a lot of talks online that address this problem: if that's so difficult, can't we do better? How do we get developers to become testers in the first place, especially when what you really want is to make developers responsible for the quality of the code they ship since the very beginning?

I tend to agree with the general idea that a tester, or a developer knowledgeable in testing, requires three basic things: *mindset*, *skillsets*, and *knowledge*.

So how do you get into acquiring or improving these three basic aspects?

Even if you can read all the books and listen to all the podcasts on testing, although these will give you a good amount of skillsets on how to test things and how the various testing suites and frameworks work, you won't be able to become a tester simply with that.

Of course, practice can help you a lot, but, all in all, the quality mindset and the knowledge of what to test are probably the hardest to acquire.

The knowledge part comes from a higher view of the product, both from the technical side and the business end. Introducing project breakdowns and pitches for the features that are going to be introduced in our software can be a starting point in this process.

The quality mindset can be the trickiest of them all, as it ends up being baked into all sort of aspects of software development from the technical point of view and requires a proactive participation from all the parties involved, first of all starting with the developer.

As previously said, there isn't a fixed definition of what you can achieve in terms of quality. There's no upper limit on how much quality you can put into your project. Hence, there's no limit on how much testing you can do in any project.

From what I've witnessed, there are two requirements that can speed up the process of becoming a good tester on top of being a good developer: one of these comes from the environment, the other comes from us.

The environment bit in my opinion is the one that could potentially cut the deal to acquire the right testing mindset that we are talking about, and getting there should probably be the priority of any company that decides that quality has value, and a measurable one.

Surely, having someone that can do mentoring on testing has always worked the best: learning by imitation and debating are probably the best team-oriented tools around. Even if you don't have a tester in your team, you might have noticed that in development, practices such as paired programming or code reviews can go a long way to keep the team up to speed with the practices and knowledge required.

Let's have a closer look at what this would mean in practice, keeping in mind that there is no silver bullet in terms of applied practices and methodologies, and it's your task to experiment and adapt based on what you have at hand.

Starting with no testing culture – a practical approach

In this series of practical examples on how to introduce testing in a team or project, we are going to assume a couple of requirements that are indispensable in getting you somewhere.

In this specific instance, we're going to assume you're working in a team. The ideal situation is to have a team of at least three people.

> If you're working with less than three people, or you're a lone developer, most of the techniques and practices tend to have a cost which might be higher than the perceived benefit.
>
> A test plan and a sound organization of your workflow (trying to keep things simple) will not only provide a solid ground for working in a larger team if needed, but also grant you the instrument to deliver quality at speed.

First of all, you need support from the business and your direct managers; speaking of direct and indirect experience, without that you won't get anywhere. The business side of the company needs to understand what testing is, in the way that is has been described at the beginning of this chapter, the value of testing, and all the good things that this can bring. There is plenty of documentation online for you to build a business case.

Secondly, you need to have some skillsets in testing. This book should cover that part—hopefully quite well—and there are plenty of others that can teach you more theoretical aspects of testing for programmers and engineers, without considering the amount of online resources available on the topic.

> A few good articles you can find online are as follows:
> * *Unit testing: Why bother?* available at `http://soundsoftware.ac.uk/unit-testing-why-bother/`
> * *Testing at Airbnb* available at `http://nerds.airbnb.com/testing-at-airbnb/`

Once you've got this, you can start moving into action.

One of the situations most might find themselves in is that there is no testing culture whatsoever. Here you have two choices: either take the bottom-up approach, and get yourself familiar with TDD as a starter, or take the top-down one, where you'll take the higher perspective.

Either way you need to start having a compact test plan to adhere to. Taking as an example the approach of ACC, you start by breaking down the application/project/library into modules (components), each of them will be composed of features (capabilities). Each feature will be denoted with a particular attribute. From there you should have a compact enough representation of what you're trying to achieve. On top of this, you can start assigning a relative risk level, which you will use to give priority for your testing approach defining what and how much to test.

The resulting test plan should be signed off by all the stakeholders and updated as frequently as possible, defining the aim of the project itself. The more this document is official the better it is, as it will be considered the business card of the project.

As highlighted by many, the immediate aim is to start planting the culture of testing in developers. Define the scope of your work, both in terms of testing and development, proceed with caution and evaluate both risks and costs, and leverage on those to take a decision on how to approach tests.

Thankfully, if you're finding yourself working with Yii and Codeception, you should be spared a bit of headaches putting together different frameworks and wasting a bit of time experimenting a working solution.

Team-wise, when the experience in testing is not widespread nor solid, additional practices can be introduced that can help avoid bottlenecks or have all the knowledge trapped in a single person, such as paired programming and code reviews.

Some companies, like Atlassian, introduced test engineers that could help the teams, both from a mentoring perspective and a mere quality assurance side. Their interventions in the development cycle ended up being confined to a more restricted participation, at the very beginning and before completing the task. Their role is, nonetheless, fundamental, as they became the guardians of the testing infrastructure, the tools, and the practices to be adopted, while the developer grew to become a fully fledged tester who can cover almost any aspect of testing without much support.

Summary

In this chapter, we've covered many aspects that are directly connected with testing, but are not strictly necessary to start testing, although they are fundamental if you want to understand why you've taken up this book and if it's necessary to go through the rest of it.

You've seen why it's important to test, some project management methodologies, how to estimate tasks and what it entails, and you've seen different testing approaches such as TDD and BDD, which will be the basis for many of the remaining chapters. At the end, I've tried to give an idea of what it takes to gain the testing mindset required to become a master in this art.

In *Chapter 2, Tooling up for Testing*, we will start gearing up with the tools we are going to use throughout the rest of this book, understanding the basics of Yii 2 and applying what we've learned in this chapter by outlining our test plan.

Tooling up for Testing

In this chapter, we're going to have an overview of Yii 2, what has changed since the last version, with which you might have become comfortable its new directory structure and organization, as well as its new features and niceties.

We cannot introduce Yii 2 without looking at **Composer**, a new way to organize and extend your projects in PHP.

Once we have had a look at all the basic tools we're going to use, let's review our plan and consider what we will be working on in the rest of this book: user authentication REST interface and user login from a modal window.

In order to start working on our features, we need to step aside and review our plan from a project management and quality assurance point of view, that is, introduce the master test plan. In other words, we need to consider what we are going to test and how much before undertaking the actual implementation work.

We will be working through the following steps:

- Downloading and installing Yii 2
- Finding your way around Yii 2
- Defining our working strategy
- Introducing testing for our purposes

Downloading and installing Yii 2

If you've worked with Yii in the past, be prepared. The new version of Yii 2 can be considered as a brand new framework, modern and robust.

Yii 2 takes a long-awaited step forward in the right direction. It is the result of several years of work, done collaboratively on the Internet, mostly on GitHub (https://github.com/yiisoft/yii2), by developers from different parts of the world.

As a user of Yii, you can collaborate too, by simply filing bug reports, feature requests at https://github.com/yiisoft/yii2/issues, polishing off the documentation and translations, and creating new extensions and features for review and inclusion on the project. There are also many other non-officially supported subprojects that can benefit from your support: some already there for you to use, and some that you may have written yourself.

Environment and workflow

As a developer, you will have your own environment with which you need to feel confident enough, and which can actually help you writing the code without many worries. If you do feel that there's a gap between writing the code and seeing the actual result, then there's something you need to fix.

It's quite important for the purpose of this book to outline my optimal environment that I will use throughout the upcoming chapters and code samples that you will find.

I will, of course, note when the environment might make a difference, but be wary that, if your environment is different, you may need to check the developer's documentation or reach out to anyone who might know the answer, in case something is not working.

My personal development environment is composed of the following:

- A robust **Integrated Development Environment (IDE)**, such as IntelliJ PHPStorm, rather than a simple code editor (for example, VIM): You get some additional benefits from it, for example, an integrated debugger, a syntax checker, a code hinting system, and so forth.

- A modern version control system (for example, GIT): Commit always and often. It's the only way for you to understand the history and control the changes in your project in a sensible way. Head over to http://git-scm.com/doc if you need more information and learn by visually experimenting with it at http://pcottle.github.io/learnGitBranching/.

- **Linux Apache MariaDB PHP (LAMP)** box packaged as a virtual machine: I've passed through the stage of having my own machine acting as my LAMP box, but this has proved to be too unreliable for many reasons. Mostly because after a while, you will end up confusing experimental plugins and tools that are not meant to be used on certain projects, potentially messing up your work.

A development or testing environment is usually quite simple to set up as it won't require an extensive configuration, as it would do in a critical or production environment.

One of the reasons in favor of having such an environment setup, in particular with reference to the LAMP box, is the ability to configure it as you wish based on the project you're working on, and in particular being able to replicate the live/ production environment as close as possible. This has a clear advantage when it comes to the following:

- Working within a team with more than one developer
- Replicating bugs occurring on any environment (for example, test, stage, or live)

Vagrant is probably the tool you're looking for if you want to start easy (see `http://www.vagrantup.com/`), and if it convinces you, it might be worth giving the book, *Creating Development Environments with Vagrant, Michael Peacock, Packt Publishing*, a shot (`http://www.packtpub.com/creating-development-environments-with-vagrant/book`).

PHP does not need major adjustments, and I believe a default PHP installation will suffice to get you started as this is the only constraint for running Yii 2. Be sure to have a version equal to or above 5.4, and have a CLI PHP available on the command line, by issuing the following command:

```
$ php -v
PHP 5.5.22-1+deb.sury.org~precise+1 (cli) (built: Feb 20 2015 11:25:06)
Copyright (c) 1997-2015 The PHP Group
Zend Engine v2.5.0, Copyright (c) 1998-2015 Zend Technologies
    with Zend OPcache v7.0.4-dev, Copyright (c) 1999-2015, by Zend
Technologies
    with Xdebug v2.2.5, Copyright (c) 2002-2014, by Derick Rethans
```

The preceding output is from a Vagrant machine running Ubuntu 12.04 with PHP 5.5 installed.

The dollar sign ($) means the command can be run by a user and you won't need administrative permissions to run it.

If you get a command not found error, be sure to refer to your distribution/OS vendor for support on how to install it. Most of the distributions provide it by default, while others require additional configuration parameters or packages.

Introducing Composer

As you might well know, Yii 1 was (initially) shipped as a standalone library that needed installation on the target environment, and from there you could use its CLI interface to create your web app. After that, the library would be sitting somewhere in your filesystem to be directly called by the web app upon loading it.

When Yii started, this was common practice; there wasn't a way to keep the code self-contained and you could easily get into several problems whenever you needed to ship the code to shared hosting environments (I'm looking at you Plesk/ OpenBaseDir restriction).

Secondly, system-wide packages and dependencies were often restricting the developers to embrace new features and work around existing bugs, without even counting that these were (too) often overlooked. If you've been working on the web with PHP for quite a while, I'm pretty sure you've experienced the sense of lagging behind other big frameworks on the development scene (and not just in PHP-land).

Composer (http://getcomposer.org) solves the problem under many aspects, and thanks to the efforts of Nils Adermann, Jordi Boggiano, and many community contributions, it was first released in 2012.

Composer takes inspiration from Node.js' **npm** and Ruby's **bundler**. It provides a way to define and install dependencies (that is, libraries), and install web applications that are available from Packagist (https://packagist.org/) on a per-project basis.

Installing and using it

Let's start by following the installation guide proposed on the Composer website (https://getcomposer.org/doc/00-intro.md#installation-nix). Consider the following command:

```
$ curl -s https://getcomposer.org/installer | php
```

In the preceding command we are using `curl` to download the installer and `php` to parse it and output an executable PHP file called `composer.phar`. Be mindful that the installation under a different OS (in case you don't have a Linux box to play with) varies, for example, under OS X, Composer is part of the `homebrew-php` project at `https://github.com/Homebrew/homebrew-php`.

At this point, you can simply call Composer directly using a relative or absolute path, as shown in the following:

```
$ php composer.phar
```

Or move it into a more appropriate position for easier invocation, as you will see next.

If you can run sudo or log in as root, move it into a system wide `bin` folder, as shown in the following:

```
$ sudo mv composer.phar /usr/local/bin/composer
```

If the preceding option does not apply, you can install it in user-space, for example, `~/bin/`, and then add the path to your `PATH` environment variable, as shown in the following:

```
$ mv composer.phar ~/bin/composer
$ PATH=$PATH:~/bin/; export PATH
```

The last command is adding the path to your terminal environment, so it can be invoked from anywhere you are in the filesystem. This specific command would need to be issued every time you open a terminal.

Otherwise, you can add it permanently, as shown in the following:

```
$ echo "export PATH=$PATH:~/bin/;" >> ~/.bashrc
```

By adding the `export` statement to your `.bashrc` (`>> ~/.bashrc` appends the output of `echo` to the end of the `.bashrc` file), you are simply making the directory searchable automatically every time you log in, given you are using BASH as shell interpreter.

If you're unsure which shell you're on, you can check using the following command:

```
$ echo $0
```

However, while this will work on most shells and it's quite easy to remember, it won't work if your shell is CSH, in which case, use the more complex but also more portable `ps` invocation, as shown in the following: command

```
$ ps -p $$ -o cmd=''
```

Once you have installed Composer, you can simply invoke it using the following command:

```
$ composer
```

The composer.json and composer.lock files

Composer works by reading the composer.json file found in the root of your project, which will contain all the requirements and dependencies:

```
composer.json

{
  "require": {
    "twig/twig": "1.16.*"
  }
}
```

The preceding snippet is quite clear: it's defining a dependency of our project on Twig (http://twig.sensiolabs.org/). This is a template engine with a clear and compact syntax. It's also defining a specific dependency on any version of Twig starting with 1.16.

Modifying the composer.json file by hand can be prone to human errors, and sometimes it might be necessary, as we will see later on, to add the packages to your require or require-dev section via the command line using the following command:

```
$ composer require "twig/twig:1.16.*"
```

This way the composer.json file will be automatically created if it does not already exist, and the package with its dependencies will be installed for you. Alternatively, if you've created the file yourself or if you've received the file as part of a project, you can invoke the install command as follows:

```
$ composer install
Loading composer repositories with package information
Installing dependencies (including require-dev)
  - Installing twig/twig (1.6.5)
    Downloading: 100%

Writing lock file
Generating autoload files
```

The normal behavior of the preceding command is to fetch the required packages as archives (called dist in composer jargon) for stable sources, or via repository if either the dist is not available or if the package is in some stage that is not stable (for example, beta or dev).

You can change this behavior by using the `--prefer-dist` option to force searching for the dist even for development packages, or `--prefer-source` to force the checkout from repository rather than dist for stable packages.

As you will see by listing the content of the directory, Composer will install all libraries into your project folder under the `/vendor` directory and create a `composer.lock` file in the root folder that will hold a snapshot of the current state of the installation, locking the installed libraries to the specific version defined in the lock file, as shown in the following:

```
$ tree -L 2
.
├── composer.json
├── composer.lock
└── vendor
    ├── autoload.php
    ├── composer
    └── twig
```

When sharing your code, you need to commit the `composer.lock` file, so everyone in your team and any other environment you will deploy to will run exactly the same version of the dependencies you have, mitigating the risk of bugs affecting only some environments. Composer will look for the lock file first before deciding to use the JSON file to download a more up-to-date version based on the definitions.

On the other hand, it is not recommended to commit the `/vendor` directory to your VCS as it can cause several problems, such as the following:

- Difficulty in handling revisions and updates
- Increased size of the repository without any benefit
- In Git, it could cause problems if you're adding packages checked out via Git, as it will show them as submodules, while they're not.

This heavily depends on your deployment policy, but, in general, it will be better to have your environments and team mates run the `composer install` command on their own.

If you ever need to update the dependencies, you can simply issue the following command:

```
$ composer update
```

Or to update a specific package, the command will be the following:

```
$ composer update twig/twig [...]
```

The `[...]` means you can add as many packages to be updated with a single command.

Packages and Packagist

By creating the `composer.json` file, you are also defining your project as a package. This is a package that depends on other packages. The only difference is that your project is without a name, yet.

Composer can help you here in defining your project/package in a more consistent and clear way. Consider the following command:

```
$ composer init
```

This will start by asking you for some basic information regarding your project, including the requirements that you want for your project, and then create (or overwrite) the `composer.json` file, as shown in the following:

```
Package name (<vendor>/<name>) [peach/yii2composer]:
Description []: Installing Yii 2 from scratch with composer
Author [Matteo 'Peach' Pescarin <my@email.com>]:
Minimum Stability []: dev
License []: GPL-3.0
```

Among these, the one worth noticing is the `Minimum Stability` option: it provides a way to control the stability of the packages. By omitting it, it defaults to stable. This option combined with `"prefer-stable": true` (or `false` if you want to have the dev versions of your dependencies) will give you enough power to decide the policy of stability of the dependencies where this is not explicitly defined.

It will then move into setting the dependencies interactively, as shown in the following:

```
Define your dependencies.

Would you like to define your dependencies (require) interactively [yes]?
```

```
Search for a package []: twig

Found 15 packages matching twig

  [0] twig/twig

  ...

Enter package # to add, or the complete package name if it is not listed
[]: 0
Enter the version constraint to require []: @dev
```

The search can be anything, and it works the same way as you would by searching on the website (https://packagist.org). If you want to have a more clear idea of what you're going to install, you probably want to have a look at the website: you need to be aware of the dependencies and browse the code to check it does what it says on the tin.

Knowing how to use the version constraints can be quite important in any project with just a few dependencies. According to https://getcomposer.org/doc/01-basic-usage.md#package-versions, the following are the possible keywords you need to be aware of:

- **Exact version**: For example, 1.0.23
- **Range**: For example, >=1.2 or >=1.0,<2.0 or use the pipe as a logical OR as >=1.0,<2.0 | >=3.0
- **Wildcard**: For example, 1.2.*
- **Tilde operator**: Here, ~1.2 is the same as >=1.2,<2.0; ~1.2.3 is the same as >=1.2.3,<1.3 (semantically: [[[[...]c.]b.]a.]x, where x is the only variable)

Composer provides further granularity when selecting specific packages, specifically you can filter by stability by adding @dev (or alpha, beta, RC or stable).

Sometimes, you are forced to use an unstable version, either because of the lack of a stable version or because the stable version ships with a bug that has been fixed in the master (dev)!

Together with require, which defines the list of fundamental packages that are a direct dependency, require-dev defines instead the secondary packages used for development, such as libraries for running tests, performing debugging, and so on. However, these are not fundamental for the application to work, as shown in the following:

```
Would you like to define your dev dependencies (require-dev)
```

```
interactively [yes]?
```

You can also skip adding packages for `require`, and then add them later using the following command:

```
$ composer require
```

While for `require-dev`, at least with the version I've got installed at the time of writing this book, you need to add them manually as seen at the beginning.

At this point of the process, you'll be able to review the JSON that will be written before confirming it, as shown in the following:

```json
{
    "name": "peach/composer",
    "description": "A Composer project",
    "require": {
        "twig/twig": "@dev"
    },
    "license": "GPL-3.0",
    "authors": [
        {
            "name": "Matteo 'Peach' Pescarin",
            "email": "my@email.com"
        }
    ],
    "minimum-stability": "dev"
}
```

```
Do you confirm generation [yes]?
Would you like the vendor directory added to your .gitignore [yes]?
$
```

Once you've got your `composer.json` file created, you can edit it and tweak it to your liking. There are many other options that can be specified. Refer to https://getcomposer.org/doc/04-schema.md.

By compiling your `composer.json` file, you are actually creating a package yourself that could be shared on Packagist with other developers.

The process itself is not particularly difficult, as you just need to add a few additional options, as defined in the JSON schema documentation (`https://getcomposer.org/doc/04-schema.md#the-composer-json-schema`), and publish your code using a Git, subversion or mercurial repository. You can also decide to publish just a dist package. Refer to the documentation at `https://getcomposer.org/doc/` for more information if you want to take a step in this direction.

Once you've created your `composer.json` file, you can start installing all the dependencies as follows:

```
$ composer install --prefer-dist
```

Composer lets you decide how to fetch all the requirements and, in this particular case, we gave preference to dist files when available. The result is the following:

```
Loading composer repositories with package information
Installing dependencies (including require-dev)
  - Installing twig/twig (dev-master 72aa82b)
    Downloading: 100%


Writing lock file
Generating autoload files
$
```

Creating your first web app

At this point, you should have gained enough confidence with Composer to be able to undertake the next step. But before doing this, forget what you've learned!

Creating a `composer.json` file and requiring a bunch of packages can be done by anyone. With Composer, you can create a project from a given package. This means that the package will be extracted into a specified directory (not `/vendor` anymore). This new project will have all its dependencies checked out and saved within its scope, that is, within its own directory.

The syntax for the command we're going to use to install Yii 2 and start working with it is the following:

```
composer create-project vendor/project target-directory
```

Here, `vendor/project` is the Packagist name of the project, in our case, the name will be `yiisoft/yii2-app-basic`, as we will see later, and `target-directory` is where you want to install it. This command won't create a `composer.json` file, so you can run it from anywhere in your environment, just be sure to specify the correct target path.

Yii 2 developers have shared two packages that contain an initial application you can start working with: a *basic* and an *advanced* one.

The difference between the two is the type of dependencies and what's already been implemented.

Both projects come with a `README.md` file in Markdown format, which you can read to understand the details. To keep it short:

- **Basic**: As the name says, it's a basic implementation, very close to what you would get by installing Yii 1, ready to be used with a default Apache or Nginx installation.

- **Advanced**: This is a very basic configuration if you need to build a multitiered application. The one you will get with the advanced app consists of a frontend, a backend, and a console application, all as separate Yii applications with some common components. It would require a specific initialization, so refer to the `README.md` file for details.

> The advanced application features an additional script called `init`, which wraps Composer and enables or disables the installation of `require-dist`.
>
> For a more detailed guide, check out the documentation at `http://www.yiiframework.com/doc-2.0/guide-tutorial-advanced-app.html`.

Consider the following command:

```
$ composer create-project --prefer-dist --stability=dev yiisoft/yii2-app-basic basic
```

We are now installing into `/basic` the `yiisoft/yii2-app-basic` package. There are other ways to get you started, but this is definitely the most clean way I can think of, as you won't be tied to a repository nor anything else.

There is no interaction required after this command, as it would carry on installing the required packages including `require-dev`.

It might be that at this point, Composer will fail in installing some dependencies, or you can fall in some runtime errors later on, so it's probably better if you check your requirements are met by opening the requirement script in your browser, which will check that everything is all right. The file is found in the root of the project and it's called requirements.php.

In Ubuntu, there are some packages you might want to install, which are going to be needed, such as php5-mcrypt, php5-xsl, and php5-xdebug. Each Linux distribution ships these PHP extensions in different ways and their naming might be different; please consult your Linux distro documentation if you're having problems on how to find, install, or configure them.

At the end of the installation process, you will note some additional work being done, as shown in the following:

```
Generating autoload files
Setting writable: runtime ...done
Setting writable: web/assets ...done
Setting executable: yii ...done
$
```

If you had memory of the previous version of Yii, this was something many were looking for.

 Please note that these steps need to be replicated manually if you're running Composer on a freshly checked out application, or you would need to run the init tool if you've got the advanced application installed.

The CLI command line

In Yii 2, Composer is used both as a way to install the basic skeleton of your web app, something you would have done with Yii 1 using the CLI interface instead, as shown in the following sequence of commands, and as a way to manage the dependencies of your projects:

```
$ cd protected/
$ ./yiic webapp ~/public_html/myproject
```

As you can imagine, the scope and functionality of the command line is now quite different and has been expanded.

First of all, the CLI is now found in the root of the project and it's called yii, as shown here:

```
$ ./yii
```

By just running the preceding command, you will get a list of possible commands, as shown in the following:

```
- asset      Allows you to combine and compress your JavaScript and CSS
files.
- cache      Allows you to flush cache.
- fixture    Manages loading and unloading fixtures.
- hello      This command echoes the first argument that you have entered.
- help       Provides help information about console commands.
- message    Extracts messages to be translated from source files.
- migrate    Manages application migrations.


To see the help of each command, enter:


  yii help <command-name>
$
```

The ones you will recognize from Yii 1 are migrate and message, which accomplish the same operations you were used to, albeit some have been improved. The only real difference is the way you'll be calling its specific actions (for example, migrate/create).

The shell and web app commands have now been replaced with a cache management tool called cache, a fixtures creation tool called fixture, which we'll see later on, and a demo command called hello, which you can use as inspiration to code one yourself (for example, to create cronjob tasks).

Finding your way around Yii 2

Now you should have everything you need installed on your box, so let's start looking around and see how Yii 2 is organized so that we will know where to put our hands when needed.

Remember, there's always a README.md file you can consult: in the advanced application, it will show you the structure and use of the various directories.

By just listing the content of the root of the project, you will immediately spot a big difference:

```
$ tree -L 1 -d
.
├── assets
├── commands
├── config
├── controllers
├── mail
├── models
├── runtime
├── tests
├── vendor
├── views
└── web

11 directories
```

I've willingly excluded the files from the output of tree and displayed only the directories.

It seems like all the content of what once was in /protected have been dropped outside of the document root.

The project structure is now very similar to what could be a Django or a Ruby on Rails application; the project root contains all the code, which is organized the same way as it was in the protected folder (for example, controllers, modules, config, and so on), some additional directories, such as for widgets, and the document root for your web server.

The directory you will need to configure Apache to use is called web, and it's used by Yii to ship only the static files, assets, and the entry scripts, as shown in the following:

```
$ tree -L 2  web
web
├── assets
├── css
│   └── site.css
├── favicon.ico
├── index.php
```

```
├── index-test.php
└── robots.txt
```

```
2 directories, 5 files
```

I tend to prefer this organization as it gives the user the immediate idea of the organization of the code by lowering down the nesting levels of the directories.

If you are keen on using Nginx, that's not a problem, and you will find the required answers in the official documentation, which can be found at `http://www.yiiframework.com/doc-2.0/guide-start-installation.html#configuring-web-servers`.

The only two directories that require a bit of explanation are `mail`, which is used to store the HTML template(s) for the e-mails (see documentation at `http://www.yiiframework.com/doc-2.0/guide-tutorial-mailing.html`), and, possibly, `tests`, which you will be learning soon.

Structure of the default web application

The basic application is composed of a `SiteController` with a couple of modules and a login system.

The configuration files should be quite straightforward to understand and can be found in the `/config` directory. We will be touching on them every now and then in order to configure certain aspects and extensions we're going to use.

Regardless of whether you are using the manually installed basic application or the Composer-driven method explained earlier, you will be required to set up the database on your environment and configure the application.

In the configuration file `web.php`, be sure to have set up the `cookieValidationKey`, and while in `db.php`, set up the DSN of your database as described in the documentation at `http://www.yiiframework.com/doc-2.0/guide-start-databases.html#configuring-a-db-connection`.

You will also note the following at the end of the `web.php` file:

```
// config/web.php

if (YII_ENV_DEV) {
    // configuration adjustments for 'dev' environment
    $config['bootstrap'][] = 'debug';
    $config['modules']['debug'] = 'yii\debug\Module';

    $config['bootstrap'][] = 'gii';
```

```
    $config['modules']['gii'] = 'yii\gii\Module';
}
```

By default, Yii 2 will provide you with a `YII_DEBUG` global constant definition, and an environment `YII_ENV_<ENVIRONMENT>` definition, which could come handy in certain conditions. Be aware that its use should be limited to specific cases where an alternative and more portable solution cannot be found, either by revisiting the implementation or the initial requirements. In a production environment, `YII_DEBUG` should be set to `false` and `YII_ENV` to `prod`.

Documentation and sample code

With this version, Yii is now following more strict standards in the way that the code is written and distributed.

Documentation and readability of the code is essential and is mainly dictated by the PSR-1 and PSR-2 coding style guide (note that PSR-2 is explicitly depending on PSR-1), published by PHP-FIG (`http://www.php-fig.org`).

In PHPStorm, it is quite easy to set up the code style. Alternatively, you can use PHP_Codesniffer (`https://github.com/squizlabs/PHP_CodeSniffer`) to accomplish the same task and validate your code:

Feel free to browse the code and check what it does. It's not massively different to what Yii 1 sample application did, apart from the use of PHP 5.4 syntactic sugar.

Defining our working strategy

Now we know most of our tools that we are going to use, but we still don't know what we're going to do with them.

Let's have a look at the features we want to implement into Yii Playground, and let's analyze the end-to-end structure of the final application and how we should meet our quality assurance requirements.

Key features to be implemented

Given what we've seen in the previous sections, the base web app provided by Yii contains just a basic infrastructure with which you can start playing around. For the purpose of this book, we're going to add several features that in a real-world environment would normally be requested by the client or stakeholders on the project through a brief, discussed and analyzed by the internal teams and scheduled to be developed.

We are going to follow these steps and outline the necessary work needed in order to meet the desired level of quality assurance for the resulting application.

As previously said, the aim of testing is first and foremost to ensure that the code we produce matches the desired requirements. Anything else outside our code is not normally tested, but here exceptions apply and it really boils down to what the third-party code is doing, its overall quality, and reliability.

We are going to aim to change the basic app in order to be able to login from a modal window.

Once you've got the business requirements in place, we would break this feature down into subfeatures, if needed.

In fact, the path we will take on how to implement the modal window and the underlying infrastructure is quite important.

The code controlling the window from the client-side perspective needs to communicate with the backend to validate and authenticate the user. On a very basic level, this can be achieved by just adjusting the already existing controller that deals with the login process.

But we can do better. We can decide to roll our new login system without changing the existing one, thus avoiding introducing a breaking change that can affect our users. If for some reason a bug will slip past our control, we can just disable the new feature, while still letting the users log into the system.

This specific feature is also bringing up a series of implicit requirements, such as security and portability of our code, and integration with the existing and upcoming functionality. We want the user login application that sits on the client side to be self-contained and reusable as much as possible. Same goes for the backend authentication system.

The proposed approach is then the following, together with the high-level assurance criteria we need to satisfy, which will outline the scope of the work in much more detail when implementing it and, on the other side, will help us create the required tests:

1. User REST interface to authenticate the user.
2. Modal login window.

User authentication REST interface

The REST interface will define some entry points to our application that will be easy to use. The URLs will then have a syntax of `/resource/id/operation`.

A GET retrieves information, a POST will store information. For example, POST user/login to log in, POST user/logout to log out, POST user/update to update some fields once if the user is logged in, and GET user/details to display user information.

The communication will work using JSON where needed.

User login from a modal window

Now let's piece together what we've done with the REST interface and code the JavaScript code that will open the modal window, validate the form, communicate the login credentials to the backend, and keep the user logged in until the browser window is closed.

As previously said, the code needs to be self-contained and portable, and for security reasons, it will not deal with any sensible information at any point, like the actual authentication.

Introducing testing for our purposes

Now that we have defined what to do, we need to discuss what kind of testing is needed and how much of it we want to test, based on the approaches we have outlined in *Chapter 1, The Testing Mindset*.

We're going to cover the following areas of testing:

- **Unit tests**: This is to achieve isolated components testing
- **Integration tests**: This is to ensure the various components are working well together
- **Acceptance tests**: These are the most relevant types of tests from the user perspective, as they try to meet the right requirements defined at the beginning

Clearly, without knowing how our application is structured, it is hard to understand what kind of work we're going to endure.

So, before getting into defining the actual tests, we need to start breaking down our application into several modules, and overseeing the structure from an architectural point of view.

There are many ways to perform an architectural breakdown, some might be stricter and more detailed, using a textual list, while others might end up being a rough sketch using a diagram. This heavily depends on the size and complexity of your application, and, in our case, a diagram seems to fit our purposes.

We need to remember that we always want to balance the effort and the time spent on these initial phases with the amount of detail required at any given point. For instance, we might not know exactly how the modal window login will interact with the rest of the application, whether we need to develop a user model that is more complex than the one we will start with or even split it into different components so as to provide a different functionality to the frontend, or whether this is out of scope with the work we want to do and we can do it in a self-contained way.

Moreover, the diagram can miss small bits, which we might forget to test or consider when evaluating our test plan. For example, the JavaScript side of our application might include several small sets of utility functions that should be considered as separate modules for manageability and reuse.

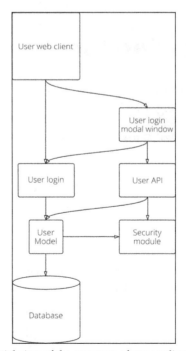

Partial view of the structure of our application

As a solution to these problems, it is always advisable to revisit the structure of the software module and its own breakdown when approaching the development of the specific feature. This is something we will see in detail in the next chapters.

In the preceding diagram, we can see that our application comprises essentially three main areas, starting from the bottom: a data storage system (database), a model representing the data, and a functional part (the view/controller part of the application). On top of everything sits our main interaction bit given by the user browser. This is not representative of the whole application, rather just the specific areas where we're going to work on.

As we've already seen, the **unit tests** are aimed at testing an atomic bit of the application, such as a class or a small set of related functions: their purpose is to be *small* and *isolate*, meaning they should have no external dependencies. Keep in mind that totally isolated tests in web development are difficult to achieve, and we are in fact not allowed to touch parts of our infrastructure, for instance, the database interaction. These tests are actually called **small tests** in Google's internal terminology , which immediately indicates their scope and the time they will take to run.

Google is currently one of the publicly known companies that have made testing one of their core values. Their approach makes constant use of adjectives to distinguish between types of tests.

To read more about Google's way of testing, you might be interested in *How Google Tests Software, Addison Wesley, James Whittaker, Jason Arbon, and Jeff Carollo.*

In our application, the unit test can be represented in the following way:

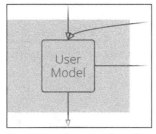

Graphical representation of unit testing coverage

A practical example is the user model we're going to create, and, as stated before, we might have other unit tests that we might want to write, for instance, in our JavaScript layer in the frontend, in case we were dealing with a client-side application where part of the business logic lives in the user browser.

Just remember, the tests covering the user model shouldn't make any use of external dependencies (for example, external helpers, such as the security module) and, secondly, they can avoid touching parts of the framework over which we don't have any control, specifically those that have potentially already been covered by other tests.

When focusing a bit more on the global picture, we can now see how things stack up and interact with each other. With **integration tests**, we might be required to use mocks and fakes anyway, but this is not highly recommended as it would be used for unit tests. In Google's terminology, these tests are called **medium tests**, as they take a bit more when executed and are also trivial to develop in certain situations.

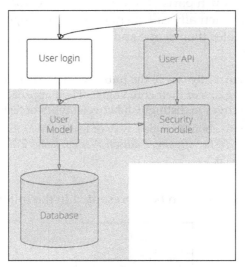

Graphical representation of integration tests coverage.

The last pieces of the jigsaw are the acceptance tests, as shown in the following:

Graphical overview of acceptance tests.

Acceptance tests are similar to system tests (or end-to-end tests), but they target the user rather than the consistency of the overall system from an engineering point of view. Acceptance tests are close to what could be a real-world use: these tests are required to ensure that all components are working well together, and meet the acceptance criteria defined at the beginning, as specific actions that outline the user interaction with the application.

Acceptance criteria are those we have defined previously when outlining our features: the user should be able to log in using a modal window.

I've intentionally avoided to use a business domain language, as we want to keep it as wide as possible for this initial part, instead we're going to dive into that later on.

At Google, acceptance (and end-to-end) tests are also called **large** or **enormous tests** because they will take a lot more to implement and to execute. They also require an infrastructure that could mimic a real-world scenario, which may not be trivial to set up. Because of this, creating corner cases can be quite difficult as this means that we're going to test only the defined scenarios and any specific case we think to be meaningful to the area that we're testing.

In our case, this might be something along the lines of "The user will receive an error when using wrong credentials."

Again, we will specifically dig into these details later on in this book.

Using a top-down approach versus a bottom-up approach

It's important to reiterate that BDD has been created as an improvement over TDD and quite an important one at that. It provides a better and more flexible language to define acceptance criteria, which will also help define the scope of the testing needed.

We have two ways to define our testing strategy and our test plan: using either a bottom-up (or *outside-in*) or a top-down (or *inside-out*) approach, as shown in the following diagram:

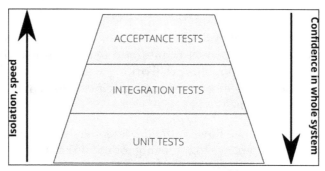

Comparison of different size of tests and their benefit.

It's not new for agencies and startups when trying to build up and improve their QA to start from the bottom, implementing unit tests and trying to get a good amount of coverage.

The use of TDD is encouraged and it's actually the first step in getting into the *testing mentality*, by writing tests first and then going through the *red, green, and refactor* phases. But its sole focus relies on the code, and the responsibility to implement and ensure they're covering the right amount of code rests with the developer.

Unit tests will help you focus on small and atomic parts of your application, and the tests, by being rather quick to be executed, will help you discover bugs frequently and improve the quality of the code developed. Your architectural and design skills will also improve significantly.

At a certain point, you will find yourself knowing that there's still something that is not touched by tests. While the project grows, the amount of manual and exploratory testing grows with it.

Integration tests can help you alleviate this problem, but please refrain yourself from spawning an incredible amount of integration tests: these can quickly become brittle and unmaintainable, especially when the external dependencies can become out-of-sync.

Acceptance tests are going to keep everything together and eliminate the need for the repetitive tasks you can perform when doing manual tests. Again, acceptance tests are not a replacement for exploratory testing and should instead focus on the acceptance criteria defined.

As you can imagine, the top-down approach gives you the following advantages:

1. A complete solution with a good enough coverage
2. A clear panoramic of the testing infrastructure
3. A good balance between effort, development, and tests
4. Most of all, the *confidence* that your system is solid, if not rock-solid

What to test and what not to test

The distribution of test coverage could end up being distributed as 100 percent–20 percent–10 percent, for unit, integration, and acceptance tests, respectively. The percentage for integration and acceptance can grow quite a fair bit in user-facing projects.

In this context, it is particularly important to understand what **code coverage** means.

If you haven't already, you will probably find some software engineer that will convince you that 100 percent coverage is essential and not reaching it is some sort of shame you have to wear for the rest of the project, looking down at the ground for you're not a respectable developer.

Reaching full coverage is a noble aim, and that's where we will try to get, but we need also to be realists and, as highlighted before, understand that there are many situations where this is not possible at all.

The "what to test" question, or in other words the scope of the testing, is defined by our acceptance criteria for each feature we are going to develop.

Using the top-down approach, we will also be able to highlight which bits are important to be integration tested, while trying to achieve 100 percent for units.

The master test plan

At the end of this initial planning work, you will have everything needed to define your master test plan.

The master test plan is a unified way to document the scope and details of what needs to be tested and how.

You don't need to be formal, and there's no specific requirement or procedure to follow, unless you're working for a big company where it's considered a deliverable at the beginning of the project to be signed off by the stakeholders.

In our case, it will be roughly defined by the following:

- User API implementation:
    - Unit test as much as possible (aim for 100 percent, but 60 percent to 70 percent is considered acceptable on a case-by-case basis)
    - Functional tests to cover all the entry points of the application
    - Well defined corner-cases — bad parameters and/or requests (for example, GET instead of POST) as client-side errors, and server-side errors handling (50* errors and similar)

- User login from modal window:
    - Functional tests to ensure we are getting the right markup
    - Well defined corner cases — for example, no e-mail specified, e-mail with no Gravatar setup
    - Acceptance tests — user clicks on the login button, modal is displayed, user logs in, user sees him/her as logged in; user is logged in, click on the logout button, the user sees him/her as logged out

As you can imagine, the test plan should be a document that lives together with the project, being expanded and amended upon necessity when introducing new features or changing others. This requirement determines some constraints that should be respected if you want to keep having a specification document that is simple enough to be updated in a short time (10 minutes top) and, at a glance, lets you know what the implied risk and importance of each component and feature is.

If you want to understand more of the topic, I would strongly suggest you read more starting from **Attributes-Components-Capabilities (ACC)** at `https://code.google.com/p/test-analytics/wiki/AccExplained`.

The ACC goes together with risk analysis and mitigation. By putting your components, their relative capabilities (or features), and the attributes they should provide, such as "secure", "stable", "elegant", and so on in a grid, you can immediately understand where you should focus your testing attentions. For each row, you can give a risk value, relative to the other features. We want to keep the value relative to avoid making it too difficult to compute and also because it is meaningful only in this context.

Summary

During this chapter, you saw many important things, which are the base of what we're going to work on in the next chapters and the base of testing from a wider perspective: you learned the importance of our workflow and environment setup, you saw how to use Composer and use it to install Yii, and, finally, we've picked up the concepts detailed in *Chapter 1*, *The Testing Mindset*, and made them concrete, applying them to our specific application and the features that we're going to implement.

Now, before we dive into the actual implementation of the application, we need to get first into the testing suite **Codeception**, the jargon it uses, and the various features that it will provide, which we're going to use in the upcoming chapters.

3
Entering Codeception

After the installation of Yii 2, as discussed in the previous chapter, in this chapter we will cover installation of the Codeception suite (http://codeception.com) and go through the folder structure to describe how Codeception works, its extensions, modularization, syntax, and the jargon used.

We will need to have a good grasp of its concepts and details as Codeception will become the main tool we will use to interact with our tests throughout the rest of this book. In this chapter, we will be covering the following topics:

- Getting started with Codeception
- Installing Codeception in Yii 2
- Finding your way around Codeception
- Interacting with Codeception

 Please keep in mind that the folder structure of Yii 2 might change when it reaches a stable release (which might be after the release of this book) and together with it, the structure used to organize tests. Always try to take notes and understand what you're looking at, since the way Codeception works and interacts with Yii won't massively change, if not improve.

Getting started with Codeception

Not everyone has been exposed to testing. The ones who actually have are aware of the quirks and limitations of the testing tools they've used. Some might be more efficient than others, and in either case, you had to rely on the situation that was presented to you: legacy code, hard to test architectures, no automation, no support whatsoever on the tools, and other setup problems, just to name a few. Only certain companies, because they have either the right skillsets or the budget, invest in testing, but most of them don't have the capacity to see beyond the point that quality assurance is important. Getting the testing infrastructure and tools in place is the immediate step following getting developers to be responsible for their own code and to test it.

Even if testing is something not particularly new in the programming world, PHP always had a weak point regarding it. Its history is not the one of a pure-bred programming language done with all the nice little details, and only just recently has PHP found itself in a better position and started to become more appreciated.

Because of this, the only and most important tool that came out has been PHPUnit, which was released just 10 years ago, in 2004, thanks to the efforts of Sebastian Bergmann.

PHPUnit was and sometimes is still difficult to master and understand. It requires time and dedication, particularly if you are coming from a non-testing experience. PHPUnit simply provided a low-level framework to implement unit tests and, up to a certain point, integration tests, with the ability to create mocks and fakes when needed.

Although it still is the quickest way to discover bugs, given the limitations we've seen in the previous chapters, it didn't cover everything and using it to create large integration tests will end up being an almost impossible task.

On top of this, PHPUnit since version 3.7, when it switched to a different autoloading mechanism and moved away from PEAR, caused several headaches rendering most of the installations unusable.

Other tools developed since mostly come from other environments and requirements, programming languages, and frameworks. Some of these tools were incredibly strong and well-built, but they came with their own way of declaring tests and interacting with the application, set of rules, and configuration specifics.

A modular framework rather than just another tool

Clearly, mastering all these tools required a bit of understanding, and the learning curve wasn't promised to be the same among all of them.

So, if this is the current panorama, why create another tool if you will end up in the same situation we were in before?

Well, one of the most important things to be understood about Codeception is that it's not just a tool, rather a full stack, as noted on the Codeception site, a suite of frameworks, or if you want to go meta, a framework for frameworks.

Codeception provides a uniform way to design different types of test by using as much as possible the same semantic and logic, a way to make the whole testing infrastructure more coherent and approachable.

Outlining concepts behind Codeception

Codeception has been created with the following basic concepts in mind:

- **Easy to read**: By using a declarative syntax close to the natural language, tests can be read and interpreted quite easily, making them an ideal candidate to be used as documentation for the application. Any stakeholder and engineer close to the project can ensure that tests are written correctly and cover the required scenarios without knowing any special lingo. It can also generate BDD-style test scenarios from code test cases.

- **Easy to write**: As we already underlined, every testing framework uses its own syntax or language to write tests, resulting in some degree of difficulty when switching from one suite to the other, without taking into account the learning curve each one has. Codeception tries to bridge this gap of knowledge by using a common declarative language. Further, abstractions provide a comfortable environment that makes maintenance simple.

- **Easy to debug**: Codeception is born with the ability to see what's behind the scenes without messing around with the configuration files or doing random `print_r` around your code.

On top of this all, Codeception has also been written with modularity and extensibility in mind, so that organizing your code is simple while also promoting code reuse throughout your tests.

But let's see what's provided by Codeception in more detail.

Types of tests

As we've seen, Codeception provides three basic types of test:

- Unit tests
- Functional tests
- Acceptance tests

Each one of them is self-contained in its own folder where you can find anything needed, from the configuration and the actual tests to any additional piece of information that is valuable, such as the fixtures, database snapshots, or specific data to be fed to your tests.

In order to start writing tests, you need to initialize all the required classes that will allow you to run your tests, and you can do this by invoking codecept with the build argument:

```
$ cd tests
$ ../vendor/bin/codecept build
Building Actor classes for suites: functional, acceptance, unit
\FunctionalTester includes modules: Filesystem, Yii2
FunctionalTester.php generated successfully. 61 methods added
\AcceptanceTester includes modules: PhpBrowser
AcceptanceTester.php generated successfully. 47 methods added
UnitTester includes modules:
UnitTester.php generated successfully. 0 methods added
$
```

> The codecept build command needs to be run every time you modify any configuration file owned by Codeception when adding or removing any module, in other words, whenever you modify any of the .suite.yml files available in the /tests folder.

What you have probably already noticed in the preceding output is the presence of a very peculiar naming system for the test classes.

Codeception introduces the **Guys** that have been renamed in Yii terminology as **Testers**, and are as follows:

- AcceptanceTester: This is used for acceptance tests
- FunctionalTester: This is used for functional tests
- UnitTester: This is used for unit tests

These will become your main interaction points with (most of) the tests and we will see why. By using such nomenclature, Codeception shifts the point of attention from the code itself to the person that is meant to be *acting* the tests you will be writing.

This way we will become more fluent in thinking in a more BDD-like mindset rather than trying to figure out all the possible solutions that could be covered, while losing the focus of what we're trying to achieve.

Once again, BDD is an improvement over TDD, because it declares in a more detailed way what needs to be tested and *what doesn't*.

AcceptanceTester

`AcceptanceTester` can be seen as a person who does not have any knowledge of the technologies used and tries to verify the acceptance criteria that have been defined at the beginning.

If we want to re-write our previously defined acceptance tests in a more standardized BDD way, we need to remember the structure of a so-called *user story*. The story should have a clear title, a short introduction that specifies the *role* that is involved in obtaining a certain *result* or *effect*, and the *value* that this will reflect. Following this, we will then need to specify the various scenarios or *acceptance criteria*, which are defined by outlining the initial *scenario*, the *trigger event*, and the *expected outcome* in one or more clauses.

Let's discuss login using a modal window, which is one of the two features we are going to implement in our application.

Story title – successful user login

I, as an acceptance tester, want to log in into the application from any page.

- **Scenario 1**: Log in from the homepage
    1. I am on the homepage.
    2. I click on the login link.
    3. I enter my username.
    4. I enter my password.
    5. I press submit.
    6. The login link now reads "logout (<username>)" and I'm still on the homepage.

- **Scenario 2**: Log in from a secondary page

     1. I am on a secondary page.
     2. I click on the login link.
     3. I enter my username.
     4. I enter my password.
     5. I press Submit.
     6. The login link now reads "logout (<username>)" and I'm still on the secondary page.

As you might have noticed I am limiting the preceding example to successful cases. There is more than this, and we will discuss in more detail all the relevant stories and scenarios before we implement the actual features further on in this book.

The preceding story can be immediately translated into something along the lines of the following code:

```
// SuccessfulLoginAcceptanceTest.php

$I = new AcceptanceTester($scenario);
$I->wantTo("login into the application from any page");

// scenario 1
$I->amOnPage("/");
$I->click("login");
$I->fillField("username", $username);
$I->fillField("password", $password);
$I->click("submit");
$I->canSee("logout (".$username.")");
$I->seeInCurrentUrl("/");

// scenario 2
$I->amOnPage("/");
$I->click("about");
$I->seeLink("login");
$I->click("login");
$I->fillField("username", $username);
$I->fillField("password", $password);
$I->click("submit");
$I->canSee("logout (".$username.")");
$I->amOnPage("about");
```

As you can see this is totally straightforward and easy to read, to the point that anyone in the business should be able to write any case scenario (this is an overstatement, but you get the idea).

Clearly, the only thing that is needed to understand is what the `AcceptanceTester` is able to do: The class generated by the `codecept build` command can be found in `tests/codeception/acceptance/AcceptanceTester.php`, which contains all the available methods. You might want to skim through it if you need to understand how to assert a particular condition or perform an action on the page. The online documentation available at `http://codeception.com/docs/04-AcceptanceTests` will also give you a more readable way to get this information.

Don't forget that at the end `AcceptanceTester` is just a name of a class, which is defined in the YAML file for the specific test type:

```
$ grep class tests/codeception/acceptance.suite.yml

class_name: AcceptanceTester
```

Acceptance tests are the topmost level of tests, as some sort of high-level user-oriented integration tests. Because of this, acceptance tests end up using an almost real environment, where no mocks or fakes are required. Clearly, we would need some sort of initial state that we can revert to, particularly if we're causing actions that modify the state of the database.

As per Codeception documentation, we could have used a snapshot of the database to be loaded at the beginning of each test. Unfortunately, I didn't have much luck in finding this feature working. So later on, we'll be forced to use the fixtures. Everything will then make more sense.

When we will write our acceptance tests, we will also explore the various modules that you can also use with it, such as PHPBrowser and Selenium WebDriver and their related configuration options.

FunctionalTester

As we said earlier, `FunctionalTester` represents our character when dealing with functional tests.

You might think of functional tests as a way to leverage on the correctness of the implementation from a higher standpoint.

The way to implement functional tests bears the same structure as that of acceptance tests, to the point that most of the time the code we've written for an acceptance test in Codeception can be easily swapped with that for a functional test, so you might ask yourself: "where are the differences?"

It must be noted that the concept of functional tests is something specific to Codeception and can be considered almost the same as that of integration tests for the mid-layer of your application.

The most important thing is that functional tests do not require a web server to run, and they're called **headless**: For this reason, they are not only quicker than acceptance tests, but also less "real" with all the implications of running on a specific environment. And it's not the case that the acceptance tests provided by default by the basic application are, almost, the same as the functional tests.

Because of this, and as highlighted in *Chapter 2, Tooling up for Testing*, we will end up having more functional tests that will cover more use cases for specific parts of our application.

`FunctionalTester` is somehow setting the `$_GET`, `$_POST` and `$_REQUEST` variables and running the application from within a test. For this reason, Codeception ships with modules that let it interact with the underlying framework, be it Symfony2, Laravel4, Zend, or, in our case, Yii 2.

In the configuration file, you will notice the module for Yii 2 already enabled:

```
# tests/functional.suite.yml

class_name: FunctionalTester
modules:
    enabled:
        - Filesystem
        - Yii2
# ...
```

`FunctionalTester` has got a better understanding of the technologies used although he might not have the faintest idea of how the various features he's going to test have been implemented in detail; he just knows the specifications.

This makes a perfect case for the functional tests to be owned or written by the developers or anyone that is close to the knowledge of how the various features have been exposed for general consumption.

The base functionality of the REST application, exposed through the API, will also be heavily tested, and in this case, we will have the following scenarios:

- I can use POST to send correct authentication data and will receive a JSON containing the successful authentication
- I can use POST to send bad authentication data and will receive a JSON containing the unsuccessful authentication

- After a correct authentication, I can use GET to retrieve the user data
- After a correct authentication, I will receive an error when doing a GET for a user stating that it's me
- I can use POST to send my updated hashed password
- Without a correct authentication, I cannot perform any of the preceding actions

The most important thing to remember is that at the end of each test, it's your responsibility to keep the memory clean: The PHP application will not terminate after processing a request. All requests happening in the same memory container are not isolated.

 If you see your tests failing for some unknown reason when they shouldn't, try to execute a single test separately.

UnitTester

I've left `UnitTester` for the end as it's a very special guy. For all we know, until now, Codeception must have used some other framework to cover unit tests, and we're pretty much sure that PHPUnit is the only candidate to achieve this. If any of you have already worked with PHPUnit, you will remember the learning curve together with the initial problem of understanding its syntax and performing even the simplest of tasks.

I found that most developers have a love-and-hate relationship with PHPUnit: either you learn its syntax or you spend half of the time looking at the manual to get to a single point. And I won't blame you.

We will see that Codeception will come to our aid once again if we're struggling with tests: remember that these unit tests are the simplest and most atomic part of the work we're going to test. Together with them come the integration tests that cover the interaction of different components, most likely with the use of fake data and fixtures.

As we will see in *Chapter 4, Isolated Component Testing with PHPUnit*, if you're used to working with PHPUnit, you won't find any particular problems writing tests; otherwise, you can make use of `UnitTester` and implement the same tests by using the Verify and Specify syntax.

`UnitTester` assumes a deep understanding of the signature and how the infrastructure and framework work, so these tests can be considered the cornerstone of testing.

They are super fast to run, compared to any other type of test, and they should also be relatively easy to write.

You can start with adequately simple assertions and move to data providers before needing to deal with fixtures. More of this is covered in the following chapter.

Other features provided by Codeception

On top of the types of tests, Codeception provides some more aids to help you organize, modularize, and extend your test code.

As we've seen, functional and acceptance tests have a very plain and declarative structure, and all the code and the scenarios related to specific acceptance criteria are kept in the same file at the same level and these are executed linearly.

In most of the situations, as it is in our case, this is good enough, but when your code starts growing and the number of components and features become more and more complex, the list of scenarios and steps to perform an acceptance or functional test can be quite lengthy.

Further, some tests might end up depending on others, so you might want to start considering writing more compact scenarios and promote code reuse throughout your tests or split your test into two or more tests.

If you feel your code needs a better organization and structure, you might want to start generating CEST classes instead of normal tests, which are called CEPT instead.

A CEST class groups the scenarios all together as methods as highlighted in the following snippet:

```php
<?php
// SuccessfulLoginCest.php

class SuccessfulLoginCest
{
    public function _before(\Codeception\Event\TestEvent $event) {}

    Codeception\Event\TestEvent $event

     public function _fail(Codeception\Event\TestEvent $event) {}

    // tests
    public function loginIntoTheApplicationTest(\AcceptanceTester $I)
    {
```

```
                 $I->wantTo("login into the application from any page");
                 $I->amOnPage("/");
                 $I->click("login");
                 $I->fillField("username", $username);
                 $I->fillField("password", $password);
                 $I->click("submit");
                 $I->canSee("logout (".$username.")");
                 $I->seeInCurrentUrl("/");
                 // ...
        }
  }
  ?>
```

Any method that is not preceded by the underscore is considered a test, and the reserved methods _before and _after are executed at the beginning and at the end of the list of tests contained in the test class, while the _fail method is used as a cleanup method in case of failure.

This alone might not be enough, and you can use document annotations to create reusable code to be run before and after the tests with the use of @before <methodName> and @after <methodName>.

You can also be stricter and require a specific test to pass before any other by using the document annotation @depends <methodName>.

We're going to use some of these document annotations, but before we start installing Codeception, I'd like to highlight two more features: **PageObjects** and **StepObjects**.

- The PageObject is a common pattern amongst test automation engineers. It represents a web page as a class, where its DOM elements are properties of the class, and methods instead provide some basic interactions with the page. The main reason for using PageObjects is to avoid hardcoding CSS and XPATH locators in your tests. Yii provides some example implementation of the PageObjects used in /tests/codeception/_pages.

- StepObject is another way to promote code reuse in your tests: It will define some common actions that can be used in several tests. Together with PageObjects, StepObjects can become quite powerful. StepObject extends the Tester class and can be used to interact with the PageObject. This way your tests will become less dependent on a specific implementation and will save you the cost of refactoring when the markup and the way to interact with each component in the page changes.

For future reference, you can find all of these in the Codeception documentation in the section regarding the advanced use at `http://codeception.com/docs/07-AdvancedUsage` together with other features, like grouping and an interactive console that you can use to test your scenarios at runtime.

Installing Codeception in Yii 2

Now that we've seen what we can theoretically do with Codeception, let's move on and install it.

Yii comes with its own Codeception extension that provides a base class for unit tests (`yii\codeception\TestCase`), a class for tests that require database interaction (`yii\codeception\DbTestCase`), and a base class for Codeception page objects (`yii\codeception\BasePage`).

As usual, our preferred method is using Composer:

```
$ composer require "codeception/codeception: 2.0.*" --prefer-dist --dev
```

There's a specific reason to use `-prefer-dist`; if you're using Git, you can get into a hairy situation with Git submodules (but again excluding the `/vendor` folder should solve most of these problems). To avoid repeating it every time we use Composer, just add the following to your `composer.json` file:

```
// composer.json

{
    "config": {
        "preferred-install": "dist"
    }
}
```

Also, remember that using `composer install` will not work if you've added the component manually to your `composer.json` file as it would consider it a mismatch and raise an error. To install the package, you need to run `composer update` either for all the packages you have installed, or specifically with this:

```
$ composer update codeception/codeception
```

As highlighted before, you might also be interested in two additional packages `codeception/specify` and `codeception/verify`. These two packages provide a further level of abstraction that allows you to write more human readable tests by using a business-oriented syntax, close to what BDD definitions will look like.

Your `composer.json` file will contain the following:

```
// composer.json

{
    "require-dev": {
        "yiisoft/yii2-codeception": "*",
        "yiisoft/yii2-debug": "*",
        "yiisoft/yii2-gii": "*",
        "codeception/codeception": "2.0.*",
        "codeception/specify": "*",
        "codeception/verify": "*"
    }
}
```

Finding your way around Codeception

All our tests are available within the `/tests/codeception` folder. In version 2.0 this folder contains directly all the suites and configuration files needed by them and Codeception as well. The following configuration steps are based on this structure.

By listing the content of the `/tests` folder, we will see the main Codeception configuration file, while each single suite has its own configuration file inside of the `/tests/codeception` folder, which we can modify accordingly to override or further configure our tests. Starting from our `/tests` folder, the following are the configuration files we will be dealing with:

- `codeception.yml`: This is for all the suites and Codeception in general
- `codeception/acceptance.suite.yml`: This is for the acceptance tests
- `codeception/functional.suite.yml`: This is for the functional tests
- `codeception/unit.suite.yml`: This is for the unit tests

Together with these files, there are some additional configuration files that are mostly needed by Yii: `_bootstrap.php` and the content of the `config/` folder. The underscore prefixing some of these files just marks them in a way such that Codeception will ignore them. Keep this in mind in case you need to create new files in the various suite folders.

Within the `/tests/codeception` folder, you will find the folders containing the tests for each single testing suite, `unit/`, `functional/`, and `acceptance/`. Each of them will contain a `_bootstrap.php` file for the suite, the actual tests, and other folders for fixtures for example.

The few other folders contained in `/tests/codeception` are as follows:

- `bin/`: It contains the test-bound `yii` CLI command, which we will use to run migrations against our test database.

- `_data/`: It contains a snapshot of the database (`dump.sql`) normally used to bring it to an initial state for the acceptance tests, but it can contain anything, for instance, this folder will be used by Codeception in case you want it to generate (and publish) the various scenarios from the tests you've created in plain English (run the `codecept help generate:scenarios` command for more information).

- `_output/`: This folder will become quite useful, as it will contain the output of the fetched pages when your acceptance or functional tests are failing, giving you another way to inspect and understand what's wrong.

- `_pages/`: This is where Codeception page objects are stored. There are already three page objects provided by the basic application, namely `AboutPage.php`, `ContactPage.php`, and `LoginPage.php`. We will explore this part further down the line as they will prove to be extremely useful as they simplify our lives quite substantially and promote modularity and reuse of code.

- `_support/`: This is used for additional support files, which currently hold the `FixtureHelper` class used to populate the database with the provided fixtures.

Configuring Codeception

Now, we should pretty much know where all the configuration files live, so we're going to review their content and adjust it before we can start interacting with Codeception and first run all the provided tests and then our own tests.

Let's start with the YAML configuration files for the different suites.

The acceptance tests are configured by default to use PHPBrowser. We will see how things need to be adjusted to use Selenium WebDriver, but generally speaking, both tools require at least a URL to access our application:

```
# tests/codeception/acceptance.suite.yml

class_name: AcceptanceTester
```

```
modules:
    enabled:
        - PhpBrowser
    config:
        PhpBrowser:
            url: 'http://basic.yii2.sandbox'
```

The default URL is `http://localhost:8080`, which you won't need to change when, for instance, you're using Vagrant or the PHP built-in server. In the preceding example, I've set up a custom domain name; this is not required in order to run your tests as it might require additional configuration steps that won't be needed, unless you're in a larger environment and your configuration is a bit more complex (for instance in case your tests are being executed remotely). We'll see more of this in the final chapters.

Please also note that you don't need to specify the entry file, `index-test.php`, as you want Yii to resolve the routing for you.

The base URL for our application isn't needed for our functional tests, as I highlighted before. In fact what Codeception cares about for our functional tests is the entry script for the application: all the functionality is provided by the `yii2-codeception` package (which should come pre-installed in your application), so in the configuration file, you have just a reference pointing to the configuration of your test application:

```
# tests/codeception/functional.suite.yml
...
modules:
    config:
        Yii2:
            configFile: 'codeception/config/functional.php'
```

Heading over to this file, we will find that at the very beginning we have a couple of `$_SERVER` variables set:

```
// tests/codeception/config/functional.php
...
// set correct script paths
$_SERVER['SCRIPT_FILENAME'] = YII_TEST_ENTRY_FILE;
$_SERVER['SCRIPT_NAME'] = YII_TEST_ENTRY_URL;
```

These two constants have been defined in the overall Yii bootstrap file:

```
// tests/codeception/_bootstrap.php
```

```
defined('YII_TEST_ENTRY_URL') or define('YII_TEST_ENTRY_URL',
    parse_url(\Codeception\Configuration::config()['config']
    ['test_entry_url'], PHP_URL_PATH));

defined('YII_TEST_ENTRY_FILE') or define('TEST_TEST_ENTRY_FILE',
    dirname(__DIR__) . '/web/index-test.php');
```

In other words, the entry file is always the one found in /web/index-test.php while the URL can be configured in the main configuration file:

```
// tests/codeception.yml
...
config:
    test_entry_url: https://basic.yii2.sandbox/index-test.php
```

 Remember to adjust the hostname to the one you will use, or leave the default, which is localhost:8080.

For unit tests, there isn't much to be configured, as Codeception is just wrapping around PHPUnit, and the two packages, *verify* and *specify*, will work out of the box.

The only thing left to update is the configuration of the database: as we said earlier, currently, you can simply update the DSN in /tests/codeception/config/config.php, in the same way that the main Yii database configuration is defined.

Tests available in Yii 2

Compared to what Yii 1 was offering, Yii 2 now comes with examples of working tests for any suite of tests available. This is a great thing as it would help us understand how to structure and implement our tests.

Once we've got the server running and all the configuration set up properly, we can just run the following command:

```
$ cd tests
$ ../vendor/bin/codecept run
```

This will run all the tests and see them passing. At the end, you will see a nice summary:

```
...
Time: 6.92 seconds, Memory: 35.75Mb

OK (12 tests, 60 assertions)
$
```

The tests provided for acceptance and functional tests are quite self-explanatory; they're basically ensuring the four pages, namely the homepage, the about page, the contact page and the login page, available in the basic application work as expected.

These tests are exactly the same, with the only difference that acceptance tests take into consideration the ability for you to run the tests via Selenium and include specific directives for it:

```
// tests/functional/ContactCept.php
...
if (method_exists($I, 'wait')) {
    $I->wait(3); // only for selenium
}
...
```

This is just an example, and it shouldn't really matter to you right now, as we're going to see how Selenium WebDriver works in detail further down the line in *Chapter 7, Having Fun Doing Browser Testing*.

The unit tests shipped by Yii 2 are the ones that are unsurprisingly different; they mostly cover integration tests between various components, for instance, for the login form and the contact form, while they leave to us the burden of implementing any test for the user. We will get there, in the next chapter.

The only thing worth noticing in the unit tests is that they make use of *Specify* for a more declarative way to write units, instead of the more common PHPUnit syntax. Again, this is just syntactic sugar and it might be easier for you to start with it.

Interacting with Codeception

So far, we've seen two arguments of the `codecept` command:

- `build`: This is used for building the "testers" and any additional code when using any additional module
- `run`: This is used to execute the tests

There are a few parameters you can invoke `run` with that I'd like to bring to your attention, as these will come handy when running and debugging the tests. The syntax of the `run` command is as follows:

```
$ vendor/bin/codecept run [options] [suite] [test]
```

First of all, you can run a specific suite, such as unit, acceptance, or functional, or be more specific and run a single test file, for example:

```
$ ../vendor/bin/codecept run acceptance LoginCept.php
...
Time: 3.35 seconds, Memory: 13.75Mb


OK (1 test, 5 assertions)
```

In the preceding command, you can also use the `--steps` option, which is a way to be more verbose showing all the single steps taken by your tests while running them.

Alternatively, you also have `--debug`, which will not only show the steps taken by your application, but also display what's happening behind the scenes, such as the POST request of data to a specific URL, the loading of a page, or the list of cookies set.

Creating tests

While running tests and seeing them passing will be all you care about once you've written your tests, you first need to write them.

Codeception helps us get started by providing a code generation argument on the command line:

- `generate:cept`: This is used for generating CEPT tests
- `generate:cest`: This is used for generating CEST tests
- `generate:phpunit`: This is used for generating PHPUnit tests, without the Codeception additions
- `generate:test`: This is used for generating unit tests

All the preceding arguments will require as parameters the suite name and the name of the file to create:

```
$ ../vendor/bin/codecept generate:cept acceptance ModalLoginCept
Test was created in ModalLoginCept.php
```

You can review these and more commands by running `codecept` without arguments.

Migrations on the test database

One of the things that I have found particularly handy and that we're going to use extensively is the ability to run the same migrations that we will create for our application on your test database.

Migrations are a concept that is not exclusive to Yii, and you can read more about it in the documentation at http://www.yiiframework.com/doc-2.0/guide-db-migrations.html.

In the /tests/codeception/bin/ folder, you will find the yii CLI command line that you can use against the test database you've configured previously to run the migrations.

Assuming you're in the root of your project, the following sequence of commands will show you how to run the migrations:

```
$ cd tests/codeception
$ php bin/yii migrate/up
Yii Migration Tool (based on Yii v2.0.0-dev)

Creating migration history table "migration"...done.
No new migration found. Your system is up-to-date.
```

The yii CLI is exactly the same as the main one residing in the root of your project, with the only difference that it will read the test configuration, particularly the one regarding the database.

Summary

In this chapter, we came to appreciate the breadth and the quality of Codeception.

We've seen the three types of tests, namely unit, functional, and acceptance, which we'll be using throughout the rest of the book. We've also touched some additional features provided by the tool and by the Yii 2 Codeception module. We've learned how to interact with it, generate tests, and deal with debugging and keeping the test databases in sync with the database of the main application.

In the next chapter, we're going to start refactoring our User class, adding our tests first and progressing through all the most important PHPUnit features.

 Downloading the example code

You can download the example code files from your account at http://www.packtpub.com for all the Packt Publishing books you have purchased. If you purchased this book elsewhere, you can visit http://www.packtpub.com/support and register to have the files e-mailed directly to you.

4
Isolated Component Testing with PHPUnit

In this chapter, we will take a closer look at **PHPUnit** and how it is handled by Codeception.

We will start with a brief introduction of the changes that we need to perform before getting into the actual tests, and from there, go through the red, green, and refactor phases to implement the tests and our code and refactor where needed.

We will introduce basic topics such as testing in isolation, integration tests of the components, and more advanced topics such as **data providers**.

The following topics are covered in this chapter:

- Understanding the work to be done
- Using the User model
- Implementing the first unit test
- Component testing of the model
- Implementing the ActiveRecord class and its methods
- Seeing test passing

Understanding the work to be done

In the scope of our work, we're going to introduce PHPUnit by first discussing the User model, how the authentication method works in Yii, and how it's going to be used in our specific case.

After that, we will sketch our tests to cover all possible uses of the User class, refactor the model, and then aim to get the test passed.

The current state of the framework that we have installed is not good enough for the features we want to implement.

As underlined in the previous chapters, we're going to follow a TDD approach for this first part.

Using the User model

Let's start by having a look at how the `User` model is used in Yii.

You can open the file located at `/models/User.php`.

The first thing to notice is that the `User` class extends from a generic Yii `Object` class and implements `IdentityInterface`:

```
// User.php

namespace app\models;

use yii\base\Object;
use yii\web\IdentityInterface;

class User extends Object implements IdentityInterface
{
    // ...
```

The `yii\base\Object` class is the parent class of all classes, which implements the concept of virtual attributes, with the use of dynamically invoked getters and setters, while `yii\web\IdentityInterface` provides the signature for methods we need to implement in our class to provide the authentication mechanism.

You will also notice by the private property `$users` that the model does not connect to a database; instead, it holds all the authentication data within the class itself. This has been done on purpose by the Yii developers, in order to have everything working without additional effort. This not only alleviates the problem of massive refactors in case you're not using any authentication in your app, but it's also a good starting point if you need to learn how the authentication works.

Authentication in Yii is not particularly straightforward, and a lot of the mechanism for authenticating a user is kept hidden from us; so, unless you need to implement some level of robustness in your application, you don't normally have to worry too much.

Instead, what is important to notice is that the authentication information is kept in an object, separate from the `User` model. This mechanism provides a separate and clean layer of security. From here, the authentication status is kept into a dynamically loaded class of the `\yii\web\User` type, which is accessible throughout the whole life of the application via `Yii::$app->user`. For instance, to check whether the user is logged in, we can do the following:

```
use Yii;

// check the user is logged in
if (!Yii::$app->user->isGuest) {
    // do something
}
```

This is actually used in several views, and it's clearly similar to what was happening before in Yii 1.

Having both static and private properties, as is the case with the `$users` variable in the `User` class, could make the job of testing our class quite hard, if not impossible, at times.

This is another reason why we need to modify the way it's defined entirely, and instead, the `User` class is extended from the `ActiveRecord` class and deals directly with the database. With this, we can make use of the fixtures that we can control without having to hardcode configuration settings or parameters in our tests, which could lead to unmaintainable tests, if not pointless ones.

Implementing the first unit test

Yii provides an empty `UserTest` class for us, so we're going to start working from there. Head over to `tests/codeception/unit/models/` and open the `UserTest.php` file.

So now our question is: what are we going to implement at this point? Well, the answer will be quite simple, once we've understood what the aim of the unit tests is.

Unit tests, as well as functional and acceptance tests, are a black box testing system: The tests will simply use the interface provided by the object and will make sure that the outputs are as expected. Since the implementation doesn't count if this changes slightly, or even radically, the tests should still pass assuming the interface remained the same.

White box testing, which is provided by code coverage, will instead ensure that we have covered all the possible branches of our code. We will discuss this further in *Chapter 8, Analyzing Testing Information*.

 Unit tests also provide support for use cases that will document effectively the use of your interfaces to anyone in or outside your team.

So, whether we're starting from scratch, adding new tests, or refactoring some existing ones, we have a few rules to help us achieve as much coverage as possible:

- Fix the existing broken tests (and raise relevant tickets if not related to our code or if the work ends up being *out of scope*).
- Implement tests for the new smallest possible unit of code.
- Make tests independent from each other.
- Name tests properly. I've started using long names to understand with accuracy what could be wrong depending on which tests were failing, for example, `testMyMethodThrowsAnExceptionWhenInvokedWithNoParameters();` you can clearly use any other naming standards, for instance, using _ as a word separator instead of the camel case; the idea is to keep things readable and maintainable.

We also want to have a few basic rules that could guarantee a 360 degree usage overview so that we can see how to use our component and spot immediately if any of its uses are forbidden, useless, or anything else. These rules are as follows:

- Cover normal usage of the class/method/whatever (positive test).
- Cover the extraordinary functionality of whatever you're testing, for example, when it returns the exception (in other words, when it should fail) (negative test).

This might be a bit off-putting, and this first step is possibly the most difficult that I've witnessed, on myself and on my colleagues. Countless times I've seen negative tests missing, creating a huge gap of potential vulnerabilities and fragility in the test.

Don't let yourself down; the reward, as we've seen in *Chapter 1, The Testing Mindset*, is priceless.

As soon as you start, consider yourself a tester, which is the first and most important step for ensuring the quality of the code that you ship, you can see what you've achieved with an improved sense of confidence in your code.

How much to care for other people's code

Not all the code you're going to test will be the product of your effort.

When working with Yii, we will start testing code or integrations with code that comes from Yii itself, or most likely as in a real-world project, from someone else internally or externally from your team.

Sometimes, it's safe to say that you don't need to test anything that is outside your scope, for many reasons. But, it's also important to understand what the implied risk of not testing these features is.

Think, for instance, about the password verification of the User model, which we will be addressing a few pages further on: the possibility of being unable to verify a saved password is something we need to avoid, as its risk could compromise the overall functionality of our application and have as a consequence the inability of the user to log into our application.

> As explained in *Chapter 1*, *The Testing Mindset*, and in *Chapter 2*, *Tooling up for Testing*, **Attributes-Components-Capabilities** (ACC) might be something you should be starting to look into if you need this understanding of the risks related to the piece of functionality that you're building.

In our specific case, our tests will be concentrating on bits of functionality provided by the parent class and the interface, such as the following:

- Validating the User model (this is clearly needed as it's a functionality that is also triggered immediately by the save() method).
- Saving the User model in the database.
- Covering the basic usage for the functions we will have to implement from the interface.

It should suffice to say that in some cases, this might fall out of scope. If we were taking into consideration the higher level of abstraction from a BDD point of view, the kind of tests we would be interested in would be the interaction with the User class, as in reading it from the database and how it will be used by other components.

Component testing of the model

Testing the validation of a model and any further data manipulation, until it reaches the database and comes back, is the basic step in Yii to ensure that the model has clear and well-defined validation rules implemented. This is effectively useful when it comes down to preventing clients from being able to pass additional or wrong data, when interacting with the system.

If you care about security, this is something you might need to investigate a bit further, if you haven't done it already.

 I'd like to stress the position we've taken in the previous statement: We're taking the consumer/client perspective. At this particular moment, we don't know how things are going to be implemented, so it's better to focus on the usage of the model.

So, let's get back to /tests/codeception/unit/ models/UserTest.php: The file should already be there, and it's more or less what you would get by running the following command:

```
$ ../vendor/bin/codecept generate:phpunit unit models/UserTest
Test was created in /var/www/vhosts//htdocs/tests/unit/UserTest.php
```

Right now, if you were to run this command, you would end up with a test that you would need to slightly change, so that we could use the Yii infrastructure. In particular, you would need to change the class your test was extending from with the following:

```
// tests/codeception/unit/UserTest.php
namespace tests\codeception\unit\models;

use yii\codeception\TestCase;

class UserTest extends TestCase
{
}
```

In other words, we need to use the provided \yii\codeception\TestCase class, instead of the PHPUnit default \PHPUnit_Framework_TestCase class.

So, let's first sketch down a few tests within our `tests\codeception\unit\models\` `UserTest` class:

```
// tests/codeception/unit/models/UserTest.php

public function testValidateReturnsFalseIfParametersAreNotSet() {
    $user = new User;
    $this->assertFalse($user->validate(), "New User should not
      validate");
}

public function testValidateReturnsTrueIfParametersAreSet() {
    $configurationParams = [
        'username' => 'a valid username',
        'password' => 'a valid password',
        'authkey' => 'a valid authkey'
    ];
    $user = new User($configurationParams);
    $this->assertTrue($user->validate(), "User with set parameters
      should validate");
}
```

As you can see, knowing what to test requires insight on how Yii works. So, it might be completely fine to actually get the first test sketches completely wrong, if you don't know how things are intended to work.

In the preceding code snippet, we've defined two tests; the first is what we've called the *negative* and the second is the *positive* one.

 Please note that passing the second parameter to the various assert commands will help you debug the tests in case they're failing. Writing a descriptive and meaningful message could save time.

 In the code snippets of this book, the second parameter of the various assert methods will not be passed, in order to keep the code snippets more compact.

What's testing for PHPUnit

Before we continue with the rest of our tests, let's review what we've got up until here: The test file is a class with a name in the `<Component>Test` format, which collects all tests relating to the component we want to test; each method of the class is a test of a specific feature, either positive or negative.

Each method/test in the class should have at least one assertion, and PHPUnit provides a long list of assertion statements that you can trigger to assert that an actual value matches an expected value, together with methods to expect for a specific exception.

These methods are provided by the parent class `TestCase`. You can get the full list at `https://phpunit.de/manual/current/en/appendixes.assertions.html`.

Some basic assertions are as follows:

- `assertTrue(actualValue)` and its opposite `assertFalse(...)`
- `assertEquals(expectedValue, actualValue)` and its opposite `assertNotEquals(...)`
- `assertNull(actualValue)`

The result of your test is based on the output of these methods. You should also try to avoid wrapping some assertions within one or more conditions. Think carefully about what you're trying to achieve and what you're actually testing.

As for exceptions, you need to use some documentation annotation:

> PHPUnit uses documentation annotations extensively to cover what's not normally doable with in-test assertions.
>
> On top of what we will see, there's plenty of other functionalities, such as testing dependencies with `@depends`, `@before`, and `@after` or grouping with `@group`.
>
> For a full list of annotations you can use, head over to `https://phpunit.de/manual/current/en/appendixes.annotations.html`.

Consider the following example:

```
/**
 * @expectedException yii\base\InvalidParamException
 */
public function
```

```
testValidatePasswordThrowsInvalidParamExceptionIfPasswordIsIncorrect()
{
    $user = new User;
    $user->password = 'some password';

    $user->validatePassword('some other password');
}
```

On top of `@expectedException`, you can also use `@expectedExceptionCode` and `@expectedExceptionMessage`, in case you need to ensure that the content of the exception is what you are expecting it to be.

Another way to do this is to use the `setExpectedException()` method, which might provide a higher level of flexibility when you have more complex exception cases to deal with.

 Although very generic, we can also expect language-specific errors when passing a different type to a method with a typed formal parameter, or when trying to include a non-existing file by using `@expectedException PHPUnit_Framework_Error`.

Assertion testing in PHPUnit is quite straightforward once you've got a grip on how your class, model, and method are going to be used.

On top of this, PHPUnit provides some clever functionality to help us speed up testing and solve some intricacies. Data providers, fixtures, stubs, and mocks will be covered later on and in *Chapter 5*, *Summoning the Test Doubles*.

Testing the methods inherited by IdentityInterface

Now that we know everything we need to in order to start, we would normally decide to implement the rules to make the `testValidateReturnsTrueIfParametersAreSet()` and `testValidateReturnsTrueIfParametersAreNotSet()` tests pass, although at this occasion, it seems much easier to just continue sketching the remaining methods that we would need to implement later on, such as `getId()`, `getAuthKey()`, `validateAuthKey()`, `findIdentity()`, and `findIdentityByAccessToken()`, plus two more methods that have been implemented and used already, namely `validatePassword()` and `findByUsername()`, both used by the `LoginForm` model.

We can immediately decide to get rid of the simplest methods to cover. We're not going to make any use of the access token, and normally, if we weren't forced to implement the method by the interface, we could have just avoided this bit. In this case, instead, we need to get it sorted and the best way to document this missing functionality is to raise `NotSupportedException` from the method and expect such an exception:

```
/**
 * @expectedException yii\base\NotSupportedException
 */
public function
testFindIdentityByAccessTokenReturnsTheExpectedObject()
{
    User::findIdentityByAccessToken('anyAccessToken');
}
```

Following this method, we test `getId()`:

```
public function testGetIdReturnsTheExpectedId() {
    $user = new User();
    $user->id = 2;

    $this->assertEquals($expectedId, $user->getId());
}
```

We can use the exact same logic to test `$user->getAuthkey()`.

While for `findIdentity()`, we can do the following:

```
public function testFindIdentityReturnsTheExpectedObject() {
    $expectedAttrs = [
        'username' => 'someone',
        'password' => 'else',
        'authkey' => 'random string'
    ];
    $user = new User($expectedAttrs);

    $this->assertTrue($user->save());

    $expectedAttrs['id'] = $user->id;
    $user = User::findIdentity($expectedAttrs['id']);

    $this->assertNotNull($user);
    $this->assertInstanceOf('yii\web\IdentityInterface', $user);
    $this->assertEquals($expectedAttrs['username'], $user-
        >username);
```

```
$this->assertEquals($expectedAttrs['password'], $user-
    >password);
$this->assertEquals($expectedAttrs['authkey'], $user-
    >authkey);
}
```

With `findIdentity()`, we want to make sure the object returned is the one we were expecting, so our assertions ensure that

1. there's a record retrieved

2. it's of the right class (`IdentityInterface` is what most of the methods interacting with the user at authentication time will expect it to be)

3. it contains what we've passed when creating it

Using data providers for more flexibility

The negative test for `findIdentity()` is quite straightforward:

```
public function testFindIdentityReturnsNullIfUserIsNotFound() {
    $this->assertNull(User::findIdentity(-1));
}
```

Implementing a test like this might raise some eyebrows, as we've hardcoded a value, `-1`, which might not be representative of any actual real-world case.

The best way would be to use a **data provider**, which can feed our test with a list of values that should make the test pass. This is quite convenient as we can tailor edge cases when it comes down to doing some regression testing on the existing features:

```
/**
 * @dataProvider nonExistingIdsDataProvider
 */
public function testFindIdentityReturnsNullIfUserIsNotFound(
    $invalidId
) {
    $this->assertNull(User::findIdentity($invalidId));
}

public function nonExistingIdsDataProvider() {
    return [[-1], [null], [30]];
}
```

In a data provider, each second-level array is a call to the function requesting it and the content of these arrays is the ordered list of the actual parameters of the method.

So, in our preceding case, the test will receive -1, null, and 30 in consecutive invocations.

If we were to use a data provider for our initial test `testFindIdentityReturnsTheExpectedObject()`, we could test whether the username contains UTF-8 or invalid characters, for instance.

So, using data providers is a good thing! It gives us the ability to use a single test to check more complex situations that require a certain level of flexibility.

But here comes the problem: The database that is used during all tests (with `$user->save()`) will continue to grow, as there is no instruction to tell it to do otherwise.

As a result, we can add the following to the `setUp()` function:

```
// tests/codeception/unit/models/UserTest.php

protected function setUp()
{
    parent::setUp();
    // cleanup the User db
    User::deleteAll();
}
```

Remember to clean up after yourself: You might be impacting someone else's test. For now, with this call to `deleteAll()` in place, we are fine.

The `setUp()` function is called at the beginning before every single test contained in the class. PHPUnit provides several layers of methods for setting things up before one or more tests, and unsetting them after. The sequence of calls can be summed up with the following:

```
tests\codeception\unit\models\UserTest::setUpBeforeClass();
    tests\codeception\unit\models\UserTest::_before();
        tests\codeception\unit\models\UserTest::setUp();
            tests\codeception\unit\models\UserTest::testSomething();
        tests\codeception\unit\models\UserTest::tearDown();
    tests\codeception\unit\models\UserTest::_after();
tests\codeception\unit\models\UserTest::tearDownAfterClass();
```

Here, `setUpBeforeClass()` is the most external call possible that is run before the class is instantiated. Please also note that `_before` and `_after` are Codeception `TestCase` methods, while the rest are standard PHPUnit methods.

Since we are here, we could also add a test-wide `User` class that will be instantiated before each test; it can be used by any of our tests. For this to happen, we need to add a private variable and add the related statement, where needed:

```
// tests/codeception/unit/models/UserTest
/** @var User */
private $_user = null;

protected function setUp()
{
    parent::setUp();
    // setup global User
    $this->_user = new User;
    // cleanup the User db
    User::deleteAll();
}
```

Now, we just need to amend the relevant tests to use `$this->_user` when needed.

Try to keep private variables and methods clearly visible; this
could also help you avoid naming conflicts, as we will see when
introducing fixtures.

Using fixtures to prepare the database

As we've seen, the data provider solution helps you run the same test with a
different dataset each time, which ends up being extremely useful. Another and
possibly complimentary solution is to use fixtures that let you preload some well-
defined data and keep tests even more simple. This would mean being able to test
methods such as `User::findIdentity()` without having to rely on `$user->save()`,
which is not a part of the test itself.

Fixtures are used to set the database at a fixed/known state so that your tests can
run in a controlled environment. In doing this, we will also eliminate the need to
delete all users in the `setUp` function or rely on static values that might be
influenced by other previously run tests.

The fixture is just a class that is dynamically loaded in the `setUp()` method, and
you're left with only the task of creating the fixture class and the actual content for
the database.

Let's start by creating the fixture class:

```
// tests/codeception/unit/fixtures/UserFixture.php
namespace app\codeception\tests\unit\fixtures;

use yii\test\ActiveFixture;
```

```
class UserFixture extends ActiveFixture
{
    public $modelClass = 'app\models\User';
}
```

In this case, we're extending from `ActiveFixture` as it will provide some additional functionality that might be useful, so the only thing we need to do is to define the model it will mimic. The alternative, as for login forms or other custom-made models, is to extend from `yii\test\Fixture`, where you have to define the table name by using the public property `$tableName`. With `ActiveFixture`, by just defining `$className`, the fixture will figure out the table name by itself.

The next step is to define the actual fixture that will define the content we want to fill into our database. By default, Yii will try to look for a file named `<table_name>.php` within the `fixtures/data/` folder. The fixture is just a return statement of an array, such as the following:

```
// tests/codeception/unit/fixtures/data/user.php

return [
    'admin' => [
        'id' => 1,
        'username' => 'admin',
        'password' => Yii::$app->getSecurity()-
>generatePasswordHash('admin'),
        'authkey' => 'valid authkey'
    ]
];
```

Each entry of the fixture can be key-indexed to quickly reference it in our tests. You don't also normally need to specify the primary key as they will be automatically created, as in the case of `ActiveRecord`.

As a last step, we need to implement the `fixtures()` method to define which fixtures we want to use in our tests. To do so, we can use the following code:

```
// tests/codeception/unit/models/UserTest.php

public function fixtures() {
    return [
        'user' => UserFixture::className(),
    ];
}
```

By doing this, our `setUp()` method will initialize the database with the content of the fixture we've just defined. If we were in need to use more than one fixture for the same fixture class, then we could have specified which fixture to load in the current test by also returning a `dataFile` key that specified the path of the fixture, as in the following example:

```
public function fixtures()
{
    return [
        'user' => [
            'class' => UserFixture::className(),
            'dataFile' => '@app/tests/codeception/unit/
              fixtures/data/userModels.php'
        ]
    ];
}
```

Now that we have the fixture defined and ready to be used, we can access its content via the `$this->user` variable (and now you can see why it's better to keep private and public variables well defined and separate). You can normally use it as an array and access the index or key you need, or let it return an `ActiveRecord` object as with `$this->user('admin')`.

Now, we can see it in action by refactoring our previously implemented test:

```
public function testFindIdentityReturnsTheExpectedObject() {
    $expectedAttrs = $this->user['admin'];

    /** @var User $user */
    $user = User::findIdentity($expectedAttrs['id']);

    $this->assertNotNull($user);
    $this->assertInstanceOf('yii\web\IdentityInterface', $user);
    $this->assertEquals($expectedAttrs['id'], $user->id);
    $this->assertEquals($expectedAttrs['username'], $user-
       >username);
    $this->assertEquals($expectedAttrs['password'], $user-
       >password);
    $this->assertEquals($expectedAttrs['authkey'], $user-
       >authkey);
}
```

This way, we can carry on with our tests without worrying about calling `save()` every time we need to ensure that a record is in the database.

This also means that we won't need to clean up the database, as the fixture will do so for us:

```
protected function setUp()
{
    parent::setUp();
    $this->_user = new User;
}
```

Following what we just said, it should be quite straightforward to implement tests for findByUsername() in the same way as we did for findIdentity(). So, I'll leave this for you as an exercise.

Adding the remaining tests

By now, we should have almost all the tests created, apart from the ones covering validateAuthKey(), which you should be able to implement without any particular problem, and validatePassword(), which we will take a closer look at in *Chapter 5, Summoning the Test Doubles*.

Implementing the ActiveRecord class and its methods

Now, we can try the tests and see them not passing before we go through the implementation of the class. So, just run the following command, as we learned in the previous chapter:

```
$ cd tests
```

```
$ ../vendor/bin/codecept run unit
```

It's very probable that the preceding command will fail with the following error:

```
PHP Fatal error:  Call to undefined method app\models\User::tableName()
```

This is because our class has not yet been regenerated as ActiveRecord.

In the next section, we will start the work of making our tests pass by starting with the migrations to move some information into the database and progress from there.

Dealing with migrations

So, the best step forward is to define a user table in the database, fill it with the data we would need, and then implement the user model on top of it with the required methods from the interface.

There is more to be said about migrations and the documentation about it is being improved and expanded every day. Be sure to head over and have a read for yourself at http://www.yiiframework.com/doc-2.0/guide-db-migrations.html.

Let's start by creating the migration:

```
$ ./yii migrate/create table_create_user
Yii Migration Tool (based on Yii v2.0.0-dev)


Create new migration '/var/www/vhosts/htdocs/migrations/m140906_172836_
table_create_user.php'? (yes|no) [no]:yes
New migration created successfully.
$
```

Now that we have the migration, let's implement the up() and down() methods as needed:

```php
// migrations/m140906_172836_table_create_user.php

class m140906_172836_table_create_user extends Migration
{
    public function up()
    {
        $this->createTable('user', [
            'id' => 'pk',
            'username' => 'varchar(24) NOT NULL',
            'password' => 'varchar(128) NOT NULL',
            'authkey' => 'varchar(255) NOT NULL',
            'accessToken' => 'varchar(255)'
        ]);

        $this->insert('user', [
            'username' => 'admin',
            'password' => Yii::$app->getSecurity()-
              >generatePasswordHash('admin'),
            'authkey' => uniqid()
        ]);
    }

    public function down()
```

```
    {
        $this->dropTable('user');
    }
}
```

We use the Security component provided by Yii to create the password. There are many other functions that are quite handy and avoid the need to reinvent the wheel.

Please note that it's important to implement the down() method correctly and test it before pushing your changes, as it will be fundamental if you need to revert to a previous state of the application, also called a **roll back**.

 In addition to up() and down(), you can use safeUp() and safeDown(), which will allow you to run the migration up or down using transactions, which in turn means that in the case of an error, all prior operations will be rolled back automatically.

The migrations are implemented and used in the same way as in the case of Yii 1, and if you've never used them before, they're a great tool as they give you the ability to define specific steps that can be easily missed when deploying your application. The syntax used should also be quite straightforward to understand and the methods self-explanatory: createTable(), renameColumn(), addForeignKey(), and so on.

Now that we have our migration in place, it's time to apply it by running the following command:

```
$ ./yii migrate/up
Yii Migration Tool (based on Yii v2.0.0-dev)

Creating migration history table "migration"...done.
Total 1 new migration to be applied:
    m140906_172836_table_create_user
```

```
Apply the above migration? (yes|no) [no]:yes
*** applying m140906_172836_table_create_user
    > create table user ... done (time: 0.022s)
    > insert into user ... done (time: 0.008s)
*** applied m140906_172836_table_create_user (time: 0.585s)
Migrated up successfully.
```

Now that we have the structure and the data in the database, we can start refactoring the model accordingly.

The Gii code generation tool

Yii continues to provide and improve its system of code generation tools, particularly **Gii**. Gii is a code generator that helps you create the basic code structure for models, controllers, CRUD, modules, and so forth, so that you don't have to think too much about what needs to be done and instead, get to the implementation part as quickly as possible.

The basic application that we're using comes with Gii (and it's defined as a `require-dev` package). And, since in our case we're running the tests in a (virtual) hosted environment, we need to adjust the configuration a little bit; we need to allow our client IP to access the tool:

```
// config/web.php

if (YII_ENV_DEV) {
    // ...
    $config['bootstrap'][] = 'gii';
    $config['modules']['gii'] = [
        'class' => 'yii\gii\Module',
        'allowedIPs' => ['127.0.0.1', '::1', '192.168.56.*'],
    ];
}
```

`192.168.56.*` should be the default case if you're using VirtualBox.

Now that we have made this change, we can head our browsers to `http://basic.yii2.sandbox/gii`. From there, we can click on the **Model Generator** section, where we can create the new model, as shown in the following screenshot:

The model generator interface

When clicking on the **Preview** button, Gii will first check whether the file(s) to be generated already exist and give us the opportunity to see the difference and decide whether we want to override the file(s) before we actually hit the **Generate** button.

Since our `User` model is so thin at the moment, we won't have any problems in overwriting it and re-implementing the needed methods ourselves. Just remember to tick the **Overwrite** check box and click on **Generate**. Otherwise, you can just adjust it accordingly with the hints given in the following paragraphs.

After clicking on **Generate**, you should be able to see the **The code has been generated successfully** notice at the end of the page.

Now let's head back to our `User.php` class and see what's been changed, and refine the implementation.

First of all, we will notice that the class now extends from the `ActiveRecord` class; this is the default class for database-facing models. There is a series of default methods already implemented, which we won't need to change. What we would need instead is to make the class implement `IdentityInterface`, as follows:

```
// models/User.php

use Yii;
use yii\db\ActiveRecord;
use yii\web\IdentityInterface;

class User extends ActiveRecord implements IdentityInterface
{
```

Now, implement the five required methods from `IdentityInterface` at the end of the class:

```
// models/User.php

/**
 * @inheritdoc
 */
public static function findIdentity($id) {
    return self::findOne($id);
}
```

As we can see, the way to find a record in the database is quite straightforward, as `ActiveRecord` exposes some very nifty and easy-to-understand methods to interact with the database. We will be seeing plenty of these use cases across the upcoming pages.

It's probably worth noticing that `findIdentity()` returns an `IdentityInterface` object. The previous implementation that we overwrote invoked `new static()`, which, in turn, triggered the magic method `__construct()` from the `yii\base\Object` class.

The new `static()` method has been available since PHP 5.3 and provides a way to instantiate a child class statically from a parent, which wasn't possible earlier. This methodology is called **Late Static Binding**.

More information can be found in the PHP manual at `http://php.net/manual/en/language.oop5.late-static-bindings.php`.

As mentioned earlier, `findIdentityByAccessToken` is not needed as `accessToken` will not be used anywhere in our code, so let's implement it:

```php
public static function findIdentityByAccessToken($token, $type =
    null) {
    throw new NotSupportedException('Login by access token not
        supported.');
}
```

The remaining three methods from the interface should be straightforward to implement and understand, and to do so, we can use the following code:

```php
public function getId() {
    return $this->id;
}

public function getAuthKey() {
    return $this->authkey;
}

public function validateAuthKey($authKey) {
    return $this->authkey === $authKey;
}
```

Left out from the obvious methods from the interface are a couple of methods that are used in `LoginForm.php`; one of them is `findByUsername`, which is as follows:

```php
/**
 * Finds user by username
 *
 * @param  string     $username
 * @return static|null
 */
public static function findByUsername($username)
{
    return self::findOne(['username' => $username]);
}
```

Another is `validatePassword`, which is as follows:

```
/**
 * Validates password
 *
 * @param  string  $password password to validate
 * @return boolean if password provided is valid for current user
 */
public function validatePassword($password)
{
    return Yii::$app->getSecurity()->validatePassword($password,
$this->password);
}
```

Here, we again use the `validatePassword()` method from the Security component, which makes the use of cryptography and any additional level of security that we want to add transparent to the user.

Seeing tests pass

As you might have guessed, it's again time to run Codeception against our `UserTest` class:

```
$ ../vendor/bin/codecept run unit models/UserTest.php
Codeception PHP Testing Framework v2.0.6
Powered by PHPUnit 4.4-dev by Sebastian Bergmann.


Unit Tests (14) -----------------------------
Trying to test validate returns false if parameters
are not set (tests\codeception\unit\models\
UserTest::testValidateReturnsFalseIfParametersAreNotSet)
Ok

[snip]



Time: 3.61 seconds, Memory: 28.75Mb


OK (27 tests, 53 assertions)
```

You should have all tests passing without problems, and you should also be able to fix them in case an error is raised.

If we decide to run all the tests, including those that were already there, we might see that some tests are not passing anymore. Don't worry, this is quite normal as we've changed the way the User model works and behaves internally. In particular, the error I'm getting is the following regarding LoginFormTest, but Codeception/ PHPUnit is quite prompt in informing us what's wrong:

```
There was 1 error:


- - - - - - - - -
1) tests\unit\models\LoginFormTest::testLoginCorrect | user should be
able to login with correct credentials
yii\base\InvalidParamException: Hash is invalid.



FAILURES!
Tests: 31, Assertions: 64, Errors: 1.
```

As I've underlined previously, it's quite important to fix any tests that do not work well. This will make us understand if we've touched anything that wasn't meant to break or that can potentially break when committing our changes.

Using global fixtures

In this case, it's quite clear that our tests have impacted the state of the database: The solution will be able to create a new fixture with the expected data for the admin user, which replicates what the migration is doing, and to update LoginFormTest and UserTest.

We will now use the default fixture user.php as the global fixture with the admin user, as follows:

```php
// tests/codeception/unit/fixtures/data/user.php

return [
    'admin' => [
        'id' => 1,
        'username' => 'admin',
        'password' => Yii::$app->getSecurity()->
          generatePasswordHash('admin'),
        'authkey' => 'valid authkey'
    ]
];
```

The previous fixture will be renamed as userModels.php; it contains additional users that we might end up adding to our application in the future. The code for doing so is as follows:

```
return [
    'user_basic' => [
        'username' => '-=[ valid username ]=-',
        'password' => 'This is a valid password!!!',
        'authkey' => '00%am|%lk;@P .'
    ],
    'user_accessToken' => [
        'username' => '-=[ valid username ]=-',
        'password' => 'This is another valid password!!! :) <script></
script>',
        'authkey' => uniqid()
    ],
    'user_id' => [
        'id' => 4,
        'username' => '-=[ valid username ]=-',
        'password' => 'This is another valid password!!! :)',
        'authkey' => uniqid()
    ],
];
```

We could have fallen into the trap of just amending the initial fixture to contain the admin user, which would have solved the problem but would have made multiple tests rely on fixtures that were designed for specific tests. So, let's try to keep things as separate and independent as possible.

Now, we can load the previously mentioned fixture in LoginFormTest as a global fixture, as follows:

```
// tests/codeception/unit/models/LoginFormTest.php

public function globalFixtures()
{
    return [
        'user' => UserFixture::className(),
    ];
}
```

Furthermore, we can amend the previously implemented methods to load the fixtures in the `UserTest`, as follows:

```
// tests/codeception/unit/models/UserTest.php

public function globalFixtures()
{
    return [
        'user' => UserFixture::className(),
    ];
}

public function fixtures()
{
    return [
        'user' => [
            'class' => UserFixture::className(),
            'dataFile' => '@app/tests/codeception/unit/fixtures/
              data/userModels.php'
        ]
    ];
}
```

Our new `fixtures()` implementation will need to expand on the parameters passed and define both `class` and `dataFile`; otherwise, it won't load it properly.

The `globalFixtures()` method is run before the `fixtures()` method, which means that the `$this->user` variable will only contain the latest fixtures and not the admin.

Summary

We've discussed a wide variety of things concerning PHPUnit such as assertions, data providers, and fixtures. We've seen how to make tests pass and how to preventively catch errors that might cause bigger problems.

There are many more things you can discover on both Codeception unit tests and PHPUnit, but what we've seen up until now should be enough to give you the confidence required to start creating tests with clarity.

In the next chapter, we'll see how to test components that rely on external code and classes, in order to get the best controlled environment needed by using stubs and mocks.

5
Summoning the Test Doubles

In this chapter, we are going to take a close look at test doubles in order to control our tests with more accuracy and avoid having to rely on interfaces we don't know anything about.

We're going to complete the work we started in the previous chapter and understand how to deal with external dependencies, particularly the difference between stubs and mocks.

We will then spend the rest of the chapter on understanding how to organize our tests to improve legibility and maintainability, using some BDD-oriented tools we've introduced earlier in the book, such as **Specify** and **Verify**.

On a high level, these are the topics that we will cover in this chapter:

- Dealing with external dependencies
- Isolating components with stubs
- Listening for calls with an observer
- Writing maintainable unit tests

Dealing with external dependencies

We left our suite of unit tests at an almost complete status. What we had left to cover with tests was the `validatePassword()` method from our `User` model class.

The problem that this method is giving us is that we are planning to use our beloved security component, kindly provided by Yii, to encrypt and decrypt the password and verify its correctness. This component is available throughout the life of the application via `Yii::$app->getSecurity()`.

The `yii\base\Security` class exposes a series of methods to help you strengthen your application. The use we will make of it is quite limited, but I would recommend reading a bit more about it on the official documentation available at http://www.yiiframework.com/doc-2.0/guide-security-authentication.html and the following sections that will cover all aspects of authentication, encryption, and so forth.

Let's then define how we think our implementation should work for this method. The documented use for validating the password is the following:

```
public function
  testValidatePasswordReturnsTrueIfPasswordIsCorrect() {
    $expectedPassword = 'valid password';

    $this->_user->password = Yii::$app->getSecurity()->
      generatePasswordHash($expectedPassword);

    $this->assertTrue($this->_user->
      validatePassword($expectedPassword));
}
```

This means that we will need to create the password hash first by using the aforementioned helper class, set it in the user, and then can use the `$user->validatePassword()` method to check whether the actual cleartext password that is passed matches the internal one. Some sort of encryption/decryption should happen behind the curtains, ideally by using `Security::validatePassword()` from the security component.

A possible implementation of `User::validatePassword()` in the user model can be the following:

```
// models/User.php

/**
 * Validates password
 *
 * @param  string  $password password to validate
 * @return boolean if password provided is valid for current user
 */
public function validatePassword($password)
{
    return Yii::$app->getSecurity()->validatePassword($password,
$this->password);
}
```

If we try to run the tests, this specific method will pass without problems.

This might be a good solution, but we need to be extremely conscious that this is not a true unit test; it's more of an integration test, as we still have the dependency on the security component.

Isolating components with stubs

The problem we are facing right now is that we don't really want to use the actual security component, as it's not part of the test itself. Keep in mind that we're working in a black box environment, and we don't know what other dependencies the security component might have in the future. We just need to ensure that our implemented method will behave correctly, given the interface of the (fake) object works as expected. We can later add an integration method to ensure that the security component actually works, but that's a completely different matter.

In order to do that, PHPUnit provides an interesting system for stubbing and mocking classes and injecting them into your application to provide a more controlled environment. Generically, these are normally called **test doubles** and the method used to create them is through the Mock Builder.

The latest versions of PHPUnit (4.x or above) suggest the use of the Mock Builder in order to configure the stub and behavior. Previously, this was done through a lengthy series of arguments to be passed to it. I won't indulge in saying that if you're working with PHPUnit 3.x or earlier versions, it might be time to upgrade!

 Please note that the `final`, `private`, and `static` methods *cannot* be stubbed or mocked as a PHPUnit test double functionality does not support this.

Stubbing in particular refers to the practice of replacing an object with a test double that might return configured values.

So, how are we doing this? I've decided to take the approach of using a separate private function to delegate the stubbing logic to a reusable piece of code:

```
/**
 * Mocks the Yii Security module,
 * so we can make it return what we need.
 *
 * @param string $expectedPassword the password used for encoding
 *                                 also used for validating if the
 *                                 second parameter is not set
 */
```

```php
private function _mockYiiSecurity($expectedPassword)
{
    $security = $this->getMockBuilder(
'yii\base\Security')
        ->getMock();
```

We start by creating the stub of our security class by using `getMockBuilder()`. By default, the Mock Builder will replace all the class methods with test doubles that return `null`.

We can also decide selectively which ones are to be replaced by specifying them in an array and then passing it to `setMethods()`; for example: `setMethods(['validatePassword', 'generatePasswordHash'])`.

We can also pass `null` to it; we can avoid any method from having a test double, but without it, we won't be able to set any expectation.

> If the class you're mocking performs unneeded initializations in the `__constructor()` method, you can disable it by using `disableOriginalConstructor()` or passing custom arguments with `setConstructorArguments()`. There are more methods that can be applied to modify the behavior of the Mock Builder; refer to the following documentation: `https://phpunit.de/manual/current/en/test-doubles.html#test-doubles.stubs`.

Any method that is a test double can be configured and be monitored with the use of `expects()`:

```php
    $security->expects($this->any())
        ->method('validatePassword')
        ->with($expectedPassword)
        ->willReturn(true);

    $security->expects($this->any())
        ->method('generatePasswordHash')
        ->with($expectedPassword)
        ->willReturn($expectedPassword);

    Yii::$app->set('security', $security);
}
```

This seems to be pretty much straightforward to read: any (`any()`) time the method (`method()`) 'validatePassword' is invoked with (`with()`) the `$expectedPassword`, it will return (`willReturn()`) true.

There are a number of ways you can configure your replaced functions: having them return only once a certain value, or different values in consecutive calls, or throw exceptions, when invoked.

 Much more is available and documented in the official PHPUnit documentation available at https://phpunit.de/manual/current/en/test-doubles.html.

We can then implement the negative test to cover a wrong password passed to validatePassword() with the logic we wanted:

```
/**
 * @expectedException yii\base\InvalidParamException
 */
public function
testValidatePasswordThrowsInvalidParamExceptionIfPasswordIsIncorrect()
{
    $password = 'some password';
    $wrongPassword = 'some other password';
    $this->_mockYiiSecurity($password, $wrongPassword);

    $this->_user->password = $password;
    $this->_user->validatePassword($wrongPassword);
}
```

For this to happen, we will need to slightly refactor the private method we just implemented:

```
/**
 * Mocks the Yii Security module,
 * so we can make it returns what we need.
 *
 * @param string $expectedPassword the password used for encoding
 *                                 also used for validating if the
 *                                 second parameter is not set
 * @param mixed $wrongPassword  if passed, validatePassword will
 *                              throw an InvalidParamException
 *                              when presenting this string.
 */
private function _mockYiiSecurity($expectedPassword, $wrongPassword =
false)
{
    $security = $this->getMockBuilder(
'yii\base\Security')
```

```
        ->getMock()
    );
    if ($wrongPassword) {
        $security->expects($this->any())
            ->method('validatePassword')
            ->with($wrongPassword)
            ->willThrowException(new InvalidParamException());
    } else {
        $security->expects($this->any())
            ->method('validatePassword')
            ->with($expectedPassword)
            ->willReturn(true);
    }
    $security->expects($this->any())
        ->method('generatePasswordHash')
        ->with($expectedPassword)
        ->willReturn($expectedPassword);

    Yii::$app->set('security', $security);
}
```

Here, we can finally see how to configure our replaced method to throw the exception using `willThrowException()`. With it, we can ensure an exception is being thrown by a method; for this reason, tests that check for exceptions are to be separated from the others.

 The official documentation provides a more detailed explanation of the use of the Mock Builder API and it is available at `https://phpunit.de/manual/current/en/test-doubles.html`.

Listening for calls with an observer

As `User::validatePassword()` is now using `Security::validatePassword()` in its implementation in a transparent way, we don't want to expose any of this when setting the password to whoever is going to use the User model.

So, we'd like to think that when setting the password, our implementation will use `Security::generatePasswordHash()` in some way, so that when calling `User::validatePassword()`, we close the circle and everything should work without having to worry too much about encryption schemes and what not.

An immediate, somewhat logical, but quite abused way to implement a test that could cover this bit is the following:

```
public function testSetPasswordEncryptsThePasswordCorrectly()
{
    $clearTextPassword = 'some password';
    $encryptedPassword = 'encrypted password';

    // here, we need to stub our security component

    $this->_user->setPassword($clearTextPassword);

    $this->assertNotEquals(
        $clearTextPassword, $this->_user->password
    );
    $this->assertEquals(
        $encryptedPassword, $this->_user->password
    );
}
```

Let's stop one second and understand what we're doing here: ideally we want to set a password and read it back encrypted, doing the related and needed assertions. This means that we are both testing the setter and the getter of the password in the same test, which, once again, defies the basic principle of doing unit testing.

As a side note, however we implement the stubbing of the security component, our logic won't look much different from the initial implementation we had at the beginning of this chapter.

Introducing mocking

Mocking refers to the act of replacing an object with a test double that verifies the expectations, for instance ensuring that a method has been called. This seems to meet our needs exactly.

In a proper black box scenario, we won't know what `setPassword()` does and we would need to rely on the code coverage purely to understand if we've covered any possible branch of the programming flow, as previously said in *Chapter 4, Isolated Component Testing with PHPUnit*.

Purely as an example for our purposes, we want to make sure that when calling `setPassword()`, we call `Security::generatePasswordHash()` at least once and that the argument is passed over to the method without any modification.

Let's try the following approach to test this:

```
public function testSetPasswordCallsGeneratePasswordHash()
{
    $clearTextPassword = 'some password';

    $security = $this->getMockBuilder(
'yii\base\Security')

        ->getMock(
);
    $security->expects($this->once())
        ->method('generatePasswordHash')
        ->with($this->equalTo($clearTextPassword));
    Yii::$app->set('security', $security);

    $this->_user->setPassword($clearTextPassword);
}
```

As you might have noticed, we don't have any specific assertion in this test. Our mocked class will just mark the test as passed once its method has been called with the specified value.

Getting to know the Yii virtual attributes

In the example we just discussed, it would have been great if we could have hidden the functionality of transforming the cleartext password into an hash from the user.

There are multiple reasons why this isn't happening, but the most important of them is that Yii already provides a quite interesting and well-done system for virtual attributes. This system is in place since Yii 1, and once you get used to it, you can achieve satisfying results.

By implementing a model that inherits from `yii\base\Component`, such as `ActiveRecord` or `Model`, you will also inherit the already implemented magic functions `__get()` and `__set()` that help you deal with virtual attributes. This ends up being particularly useful when you are in need of creating additional attributes without any effort.

Let's see a more practical example.

Let's assume that our User model had a first name and a last name field in the database, but we would need to create the full name attribute without adding a new column in the user table:

```php
namespace app\models;

class User extends ActiveRecord
{
    /**
     * Getter for fullname
     */
    public function getFullname()
    {
        return $this->firstname . ' ' . $this->lastname;
    }

    // rest of the class
}
```

So, we can access the field as if it was a normal attribute of the class:

```php
public function testGetFullnameReturnsTheCorrectValue()
{
    $user = new User;
    $user->firstname = 'Rainer';
    $user->lastname = 'Wolfcastle';

    $this->assertEquals(
        $user->firstname . ' ' . $user->lastname,
        $user->fullname
    );
}
```

Plain and simple public attributes work as you would expect them to. In the following snippets of code, I'm introducing a new class Dog, purely for example purposes, which extends from Model:

```php
namespace app\models;

use Yii;
use yii\base\Model

class Dog extends Model
{
    public $age;
}
```

Therefore, our tests would pass without problems:

```
public function testDogAgeIsRecordedCorrectly()
{
    $expectedAge = 7;
    $dog = new Dog;
    $dog->age = $expectedAge;

    $this->assertEquals($expectedAge, $dog->age);
}
```

This shouldn't be a surprise to you at all, but let's see what happens if we have both:

```
namespace app\models;

class Dog extends ActiveRecord
{
    const AGE_MULTIPLIER = 7;
    public $age;

    public function setAge($age)
    {
        // let's record it in dog years
        $this->age = $age * self::AGE_MULTIPLIER;
    }

    // rest of the class
}
```

Now, we are expecting `setAge()` to be triggered on assignment, while reading directly the value of the public attribute:

```
public function testDogAgeIsRecordedInDogYears()
{

    $dog = new Dog;
    $dog->age = 8;

    $this->assertEquals(
        56,
        $dog->age
    );
}
```

However, running this test will only reveal the sad truth:

```
$ ../vendor/bin/codecept run unit models/DogTest.php
```

```
1) tests\codeception\unit\models\DogTest::testAgeIsRecordedInDogYears
Failed asserting that 8 matches expected 56.
```

Yes, the test is exactly the same.

Having getters and setters automatically handled by our classes comes at an expense. The sequence of checks that are performed by the magic setter can be summarized with the following:

```
BaseActiveRecord::__set($name, $value)
   if (BaseActiveRecord::hasAttribute($name))
      $this->_attributes[$name] = $value;
   else
      Component::__set($name, $value)
         if (method_exists($this, 'set'.$name))
            $this->'set'.$name($value);
         if (method_exist($this, 'get'.$name))
            throw new InvalidCallException(...);
         else
            throw new UnknownPropertyException(...);
```

If you have implemented a model extending from yii\base\ActiveRecord, its base class will first check if the attribute is already available as a table column; otherwise, it will pass the call over to Component::__set(). This method is available not only for models extending from yii\base\Model, but also for any other that implicitly inherits from yii\base\Component, such as behaviors and events.

Following this, we can see that the setter will ensure that the 'set'.$name method is available in our class, and if there's only a getter, then it will raise an exception.

In our initial definition of the firstname getter, we could have had the following additional test:

```
/**
 * @expectedException yii\base\InvalidCallException
 */
public function testSetFullnameThrowsException()
{
    $user = new User;
    $user->firstname = 'Fido';
    $user->lastname = 'Smith';
```

```
        // setter not available
        $user->fullname = 'Something Else';
}
```

There are a couple or more things regarding events and behaviors done in the setter, but we won't touch them as of now.

So, going back to our `setPassword()` conundrum, we need to be aware that if we were to trigger the magic method by using `$user->password` for the left assignment, this won't trigger our method.

So, the best solution would ideally have been to call the stored password in a more declarative way, such as `password_hash`.

Writing maintainable unit tests

As the last part, before leaving the unit tests behind, I wanted to show some additional features provided by Codeception that have been already introduced in *Chapter 1, The Testing Mindset*.

Codeception has been created with modularity and flexibility in mind, so anything else is your responsibility. In particular, you might have already noticed that our `UserTest` class has grown quite a bit.

So, what would happen if a change in the interface or in the way our model works breaks our tests?

It's quite clear, especially if you're working in a team or even more if your code gets handed over to other people to maintain, that you need clear rules so that everybody agrees on how to write the code, as a starter, and tests.

I've already highlighted in *Chapter 4, Isolated Component Testing with PHPUnit*, that one of the very basic things I've started doing with the teams I've worked with and with my own code, is to define precise and simple rules, which aim at the clarity and readability of the code. I've seen way too many "developer rockstars" that show off how good they are at writing compressed code, nesting variables, and hiding multiple assignments. Writing code that ends up being obfuscated might be fun if that code is a throwaway.

Code legibility ends up being one of the ways I've seen companies select candidates, and a very quick test is to have someone read your code and be able to get what it does without asking.

Tests shouldn't be treated with less care than your application code: if done properly, tests represent a way of documenting how things are supposed to be working and how they should be used. As soon as your class provides more and more functionality, your test classes will start to grow and you need to be prepared to face a refactor and introduce regression testing when a change in the application happens or a bug is introduced.

Using BDD specification testing

Codeception provides a nice and compact tool called **Specify**, which we have already introduced previously.

With PHPUnit alone, we only have methods to split our tests; using Specify, we have another layer of organization: The method becomes our *story* and our specification blocks our *scenarios*.

Just for documentation purposes, it should be noted that PHPUnit has its own BDD-compatible syntactic sugar with the given(), when() and then() methods, as explained at https://phpunit.de/manual/3.7/en/behaviour-driven-development.html. You can still use this syntax, if you are more used to it.

As a clearer example, we can group all validation rules within the same test and split the definition of what we're doing by using Specify blocks, as follows:

```php
use Specify;

public function testValidationRules()
{
    $this->specify(
        'user should not validate if no attribute is set',
        function () {
verify_not($this->_user->validate());
}
    );

    $this->specify(
        'user should validate if all attributes are set',
        function () {
            $this->_user->attributes = [
                'username'=>'valid username',
                'password'=>'valid password',
                'authkey' =>'valid authkey'
            ];
            verify_that($this->_user->validate());
```

```
        }
    );
}
```

As we can see, we are now aggregating two of our previous tests within a single method and grouping them within two blocks of `specify()` calls.

Specify is defined as a trait; this is the reason why you need to both use the namespace in the outermost global scope and load it within the test class:

```
namespace tests\codeception\unit\models;

use Codeception\Specify;
use yii\codeception\TestCase;
// other imported namespaces

class UserTest extends TestCase
{
    use Specify;

    // our test methods will follow
    // we can now use $this->specify()
}
```

As you can see `specify()` requires only two arguments: a simple description of the scenario that we are about to define, and an anonymous function that contains the assertions we want to do.

At this point, we can either use the PHPUnit classic assertions we've used until now or try to empower BDD style assertions. **Verify**, a small and nifty package, will provide you this capability, allowing you to use methods such as `verify()`, `verify_that()`, and `verify_not()`.

From the earlier specified scenarios, consider the following line of code:

```
verify_not($this->_user->validate());
```

This is exactly the same as using the PHPUnit assertion:

```
$this->assertFalse($this->_user->validate());
```

In order to perform more elaborate assertions, we can instead use `verify()` in the following way:

```
$this->specify(
    'user with username too long should not validate',
    function () {
```

```
$this->_user->username = 'this is a username longer than
   24 characters';

verify_not($this->_user->validate('username'));
verify($this->_user->getErrors('username'))->notEmpty();
}
);
```

 There are plenty of other assertions that can be used and can be found at the project homepage at https://github.com/Codeception/Verify.

Summary

In this chapter, we've covered the long-awaited mocks and stubs that will allow you to perform proper component tests. In the final part, we've taken a better look at code organization for your tests and a BDD-like way of writing them by using Specify and Verify.

In the following chapter, we're going to take a look at the next step of implementing the functional tests that should define the REST interface for our user.

6
Testing the API – PHPBrowser to the Rescue

We are now going to delve into functional testing. In the previous chapter, we created the initial steps that deal with the user model, but now we will be creating the REST interface that deals with the user.

Before we even start to worry about the REST interface and its tests, we will be analyzing what's already available in the Yii basic app and later expand on the topic to create more awesome stuff.

This chapter is hence divided into three sections with an increasing level of difficulty, so keep your eyes peeled and feel free to revisit it multiple times until you understand each section which are:

- Functional tests in Yii 2
- Functional tests for REST interfaces
- Creating a RESTful web service with Yii 2

Functional tests in Yii 2

As you saw in *Chapter 3, Entering Codeception*, we have some basic functional tests preloaded in our basic application.

Let's start digging into that and once you acquire the required knowledge, we're going to move on to the tests for the REST interface.

As you know, the basic application is composed of a few pages, a login system, and a contact form.

The functional tests cover almost everything, so let's start to see what files we have and what's their content.

Understanding and improving the available CEPTs

The tests contained in `codeception/functional/HomeCept.php` are quite straightforward to understand. Thanks to the syntax used by Codeception, you can easily understand what the intention of the test is, so let's break it down and see what each bit does:

```
$I = new FunctionalTester($scenario);
```

You would start by initializing the actor under which the tests will be performed. Yii uses a slightly different naming than the one officially used in the documentation and guide of Codeception, which is `TestGuy`, so keep that in mind when you're confronted with documentation outside of Yii's.

> Remember that you can name the actors whatever you want, and their configuration is found in the suite YAML file, which for functional tests is `tests/codeception/functional.suite.yml`.

This class is located within the same folder as that of the other functional tests and is generated automatically by running `codecept build`:

```
$I->wantTo('ensure that home page works');
```

The very first step is to declare the scope of the test in a compact but detailed way; this will help you and non-technical people to understand what went wrong and if the test is effectively doing what it is meant to be doing in a strong and comprehensive way. The method `wantTo()` should be called only once, as any following invocations will override what has been set previously:

```
$I->amOnPage(Yii::$app->homeUrl);
```

Our tests need a starting point; the method `amOnPage()` does nothing but load the given URL where our actual test will take place:

```
$I->see('My Company');
$I->seeLink('About');
```

In Codeception, assertions are performed through `see*` and `dontSee*` actions, ensuring a particular portion of text or link is present/absent in the page.

These actions can be as descriptive as needed, and in the preceding example with see('My Company'), we are just checking that the text is present somewhere in the markup rather than in a particular tag while seeLink('About') would be the same as writing see('About', 'a'). We will shortly see that we could pass a second parameter to seeLink(), which will allow us to check the URL where the link should point to.

Interaction with the page in the form of triggering, clicking links with click(), filling fields with fillField(), checkOption(), submitForm(), and so on is all you can do with Codeception functional tests. Anything more complicated must be re-evaluated carefully, as you might actually need to move it into acceptance tests instead:

```
$I->click('About');
$I->see('This is the About page.');
```

In the preceding lines, we are triggering the link of the "About" page and expecting that the resulting page has a specific copy in it. This specific test just makes a point in using links to navigate through our application, as it could have been done as described earlier by using seeLink('About', '/about') and to leave any assertion with the About page within its own test.

We might as well extend the test a bit more and make it more relevant to what we're trying to test; what are the functionality parts that we want to make sure exist, without which we can consider the page "non-functional"? In our instance, we are talking about the title of the page (as it's already been done), the menu, and any other links we always want to have there:

```
$I = new FunctionalTester($scenario);
$I->wantTo('ensure that home page works');
$I->amOnPage(Yii::$app->homeUrl);
```

The beginning is the same, but then we ensure that the title for the page contains what we expect it to be:

```
$I->expect('the title to be set correctly');
$I->seeInTitle('My Yii Application');
```

The next section instead makes sure that the menu contains all the required links to the various pages:

```
$I->expectTo('see all the links of the menu');
$I->seeLink('Home', '/');
$I->seeLink('About', '/about');
$I->seeLink('Login', '/login');
$I->seeLink('Contact', '/contact');
```

You have to keep in mind that the links are not strictly checked; this means that if you have `$I->seeLink('Something', '/something')`, it will match any link that contains `Something`; for example, it can be `Something Else` and any `href` attribute like `/something/else`, or even `http://something.com`.

In our case, it clearly renders the check for the link to the home page a bit irrelevant, so we might well grab the current URL and check against it in the following way:

```
$url = $I->grabFromCurrentUrl();
$I->seeLink('Home', $url);
```

There are different ways to grab content to be reused dynamically in the rest of the tests, such as `grabAttributeFrom()`, `grabCookie()`, `grabResponse()`, and so on. Once again, your `FunctionalTester` class will contain the details of these methods in case your IDE does not support code hinting.

We can do the same for any other link that is pointing to the homepage:

```
$I->expectTo('see a self-referencing link to my company homepage');
$I->seeLink('My Company', $url);
```

For the rest of the links, it might also be useful to check that our routes are well configured; for instance, you need to check if the name of the controller doesn't show up:

```
$I->dontSeeLink('About', 'site/about');
$I->dontSeeLink('Login', 'site/login');
$I->dontSeeLink('About', 'site/contact');
```

The last bit we want to make sure of is that the `Home` link is marked as selected.

For this test, we need to use a very prescriptive selector as the active class that identifies the status of our link is in the parent of the actual anchor, and as there's no way to assert that in a simple way, so making use of XPath expressions comes particularly handy:

```
$I->expectTo('see the link of the homepage as selected');
$I->seeElement('//li[@class="active"]/a[contains(.,"Home")]');
```

Most of the methods available that require a context selector such as `click()`, `see()`, and, `seeElement()` can accept this parameter in various formats, mostly as CSS selectors, XPath queries or Locators, which are specific objects made available by Codeception.

In its simplest form, selectors can be just a simple word or sentence, which means "find me the first context where this word/sentence appears". As you saw earlier, `see("Something")` will return the first element that contains `Something` as its value (for example, `Something Else`).

CSS selectors are probably the ones you might be more comfortable with, but for more complex stuff, XPath is generally the winner.

In the preceding example, the XPath query `//li[@class="active"]/a[contains(.,"Home")]`, can be read as shown here:

- Find me all the `li` nodes at any level (`//li`)
- Filter them by a specific class attribute (`[@class="active"]`);—mind that is literal and case-sensitive
- Within those find me the direct descendant `a` nodes (`/a`)
- Filter them if they contain a specific text (`[contains(.,"Home")]`)

 XPath 2.0 has been a W3C recommendation since December 2010, and you can read more about it at `http://www.w3.org/TR/xpath20/`.

Locators can ease the process of writing even more complex queries in your DOM and let you combine CSS and XPath queries via OR:

```
use \Codeception\Util\Locator;

$I->see('Title', Locator::combine('h1','h2','h3'));
```

With the preceding statement, we can check the presence of the `Title` string in any h1, h2, or h3 tag.

Another possibly useful feature is a method available in Locator that you can use to browse the page via `tabIndex`:

```php
<?php
use \Codeception\Util\Locator;

$I->fillField(Locator::tabIndex(1), 'davert');
$I->fillField(Locator::tabIndex(2) , 'qwerty');
$I->click('Login');
```

 The preceding example has been deliberately taken from the documentation page of Locator, available at `http://codeception.com/docs/reference/Locator`.

Writing reusable page interactions

Testing forms is probably one of the most strenuous tasks any developer and tester has probably ever done. You can feel the pain if you think of forms as questionnaires of several single and multiple choice questions, spread across several pages.

You can clearly see the direct benefit of automating using functional tests.

The two examples already available, `LoginCept.php` and `ContactCept.php`, are a good starting point. Let's have a closer look at `LoginCept.php`; if you scan through the content of the test, you will immediately notice that the `fillField()` method is never called, and in its place we have the following command:

```
$loginPage = LoginPage::openBy($I);

$I->see('Login', 'h1');
$I->amGoingTo('try to login with empty credentials');
$loginPage->login('', '');
```

Pages are, in fact, one of the easiest ways to reuse components across tests. The sequence of actions that are repeated several times in the same test are likely to be taken and put into a page like the one used in our test:

```
namespace tests\codeception\_pages;

use yii\codeception\BasePage;

/**
 * Represents login page
 * @property \AcceptanceTester|\FunctionalTester $actor
 */
class LoginPage extends BasePage
{
    public $route = 'site/login';

    /**
     * @param string $username
     * @param string $password
     */
    public function login($username, $password)
    {
        $this->actor->fillField(
            'input[name="LoginForm[username]"]', $username
        );
        $this->actor->fillField(
            'input[name="LoginForm[password]"]', $password
```

```
        );
        $this->actor->click('login-button');
    }
}
```

The only thing needed is the route associated to it and then you can implement as many methods as you need to achieve whatever you need, which is the login process in the preceding case.

Within the `Page` class, `$this->actor` is a reference to the actor that is currently in use in the test.

You have two ways to use pages; the first is by opening the page immediately and associate it with the current actor, as seen earlier with `LoginPage::openBy($I)`, otherwise, you can simply call its constructor and load the page (also with different parameters) when needed:

```
$loginPage = new LoginPage($I);
$loginPage->getUrl();
```

Now, as you saw while working with unit tests, being able to keep the content of the database under a controlled state is very useful. And, once again, fixtures come to our help, even here.

Implementing fixtures

In *Chapter 4, Isolated Component Testing with PHPUnit*, you saw how to implement a fixture. In functional tests the same classes can be used; the only difference is that Codeception's PHPBrowser and its underlying infrastructure doesn't know how to load fixtures, so each framework using Codeception, like what Yii does, needs to provide the bridging to fill in this gap.

The advanced app provides the implementation for `FixtureHelper` that implements the Codeception `Module` class and imports the methods from `FixtureTrait`:

```php
<?php

namespace tests\codeception\_support;

use tests\codeception\fixtures\UserFixture;
use Codeception\Module;
use yii\test\FixtureTrait;

/**
 * This helper is used to populate database with needed
```

```
 * fixtures before any tests should be run.
 * For example - populate database with demo login user
 * that should be used in acceptance and functional tests.
 * All fixtures will be loaded before suite will be
 * started and unloaded after it.
 */
class FixtureHelper extends Module
{

    /**
     * Redeclare visibility because Codeception includes
     * all public methods that not starts from "_"
     * and not excluded by module settings, in actor class.
     */
    use FixtureTrait {
        loadFixtures as protected;
        fixtures as protected;
        globalFixtures as protected;
        unloadFixtures as protected;
        getFixtures as protected;
        getFixture as public;
    }

    /**
     * Method called before any suite tests run.
     * Loads User fixture login user
     * to use in acceptance and functional tests.
     * @param array $settings
     */
    public function _beforeSuite($settings = [])
    {
        $this->loadFixtures();
    }

    /**
     * Method is called after all suite tests run
     */
    public function _afterSuite()
    {
        $this->unloadFixtures();
    }

    /**
     * @inheritdoc
```

```
        */
        public function fixtures()
        {
            return [
                'user' => [
                    'class' => UserFixture::className(),
                    'dataFile' => '@tests/codeception/fixtures/data/init_
    login.php',
                ],
            ];
        }
    }
```

The preceding code is quite simple, and the only important bit is that in the `FixtureHelper`, we implement the `fixtures()` method that returns the list of models handled and their data files that contain all the rows we want in the database. The only difference with the original code that is found in the advanced app is the import of the `getFixture()` method as public, and we'll later see why this is so.

The following code is for the `init_login.php` file:

```
<?php

return [
    'basic' => [
        'username' => 'user',
        'authkey' => uniqid(),
        'password' => Yii::$app->security->generatePasswordHash(
            'something'
        ),
    ],
];
```

As we imported the trait `getFixture()` as public, we can access the fixture through `$I->getFixture('user')` in a similar way to what we did in our unit tests.

 If you need to load additional fixtures, you can similarly expose the `loadFixtures()` method from the `FixtureTrait` trait and use it directly in your tests.

The last step is about loading the module in Codeception configuration:

```
# tests/codeception/functional.suite.yml

modules:
    enabled:
        - ...
        - tests\codeception\_support\FixtureHelper
```

And after running `codecept build`, the fixture will be automatically loaded when running the tests in the `_beforeSuite()` and `_afterSuite()` methods.

Pitfalls of functional tests

A word of advice is that there's plenty of information on functional tests, as well as what cannot be tested, in the official documentation.

The most important thing to grab there is all about the underlying technology that is used to perform tests; PHPBrowser is in fact a powerful tool, but as the whole functional test does not rely on the presence of a web server like you would have in a normal client-server situation, your application and functional tests will be running in the same memory space.

 Normally the memory is cleaned during the `_after()` method execution, but remember that if you see any of your tests failing, remember to execute the test file separately, before starting to doubt your sanity.

Functional tests for REST interfaces

Up until now, you have seen what's already been implemented, what is possible to do out of the box, and some additional functionalities like the fixtures.

Now let's have a look at what testing a REST interface entails; the default functional tests available in Codeception are executed by PHPBrowser, and the interface exposed to interact with it is quite limited and can only be used to deal and interact with the markup output by the web server. The REST module provided by Codeception is something we would love.

Just to cite a few of the features available, you'll have functions to set and read headers, such as `seeHttpHeader()` and `haveHttpHeader()`, and specific methods to call HTTP requests towards our interface, such as `sendGET()`, `sendPUT()`, and `sendOPTIONS()`.

Specifically for our interface of the user, our tests will be split into two parts:

- Tests on the actual functionality—authentication and interaction with the application
- Some additional tests to ensure that we are exposing the right endpoints

Now, with this in mind, let's start having a look at the configuration part; in the `functional.suite.yml` file, just add the REST module and configure it as shown in the following code:

```
# tests/codeception/functional.suite.yml

modules:
    enabled:

        - Filesystem
        - Yii2
        - REST
        - tests\codeception\_support\FixtureHelper
    config:
        Yii2:
            configFile: 'codeception/config/functional.php'
        PhpBrowser:
            url: 'http://basic-dev.yii2.sandbox'
        REST:
            url: 'http://basic-dev.yii2.sandbox/v1/'
```

The last line is quite important, as we will end up making calls by specifying only our endpoint without the need of naming the module base path. Clearly things need to be adjusted accordingly in case you have more than one REST endpoint you need to test.

Now, once again we need to run `codecept build` in order to get everything ready before starting to run our tests. This command, as already seen, will take all the module's methods and merge them into our actor's class (which in this case is `FunctionalTester`).

Let's generate our new test file with the following commands:

```
$ cd tests/
$ ../vendor/bin/codecept generate:cept functional UserAPICept
Test was created in UserAPICept.php
```

Now that we have the file, we can start implementing our tests:

```php
<?php
// tests/codeception/functional/UserAPICept.php

$I = new FunctionalTester($scenario);
$I->wantTo('test the user REST API');
```

We start the file with the initialization of the `FunctionalTester` and the definition of the scope of our test.

Defining the API endpoints

As it's now time to implement the tests for our API endpoints, we need to define what these will look like and take our architectural decisions if these haven't been taken beforehand.

The basic interaction we want to provide to our clients interacting with our APIs is the ability to retrieve the user information, and modify it with the specific ability to change the password.

The client would normally know only the username and password. Since our update method will leverage on the ID of the user, we need to find a way for the client to get it in advance. Depending on the type of authentication protocol you decide to use, you can decide to return it right after the authentication has happened, otherwise you need to find a different way.

As you will later see, you're going to use the simplest of the authentication methods available, that is HTTP Basic Auth, which means that all our requests require a username and password to be sent along with them in a header. By doing so we clearly can't return the user ID in the response as this should contain the answer to the call and not the authentication header, so we can decide to provide a "search by username" endpoint. This will clearly make the username a unique field in the database, but that's not an issue, rather it's something you need to take into consideration if you're providing a user creation interface.

Now, we have the following endpoints to test:

- `GET users/search/<username>`: This is used to retrieve the ID of the user.
- `GET users/<id>`: This is used to retrieve any other information associated with the user.
- `PUT users/<id>`: This is used to update the password.

Implementing the tests for the API

As our passwords are passed as encrypted in the fixtures, we need to hardcode them in the tests, in order to authenticate appropriately.

This is not a good practice as we are going to make things a bit harder to maintain. On the other end, if things get more complex, we might want to refactor the code and find a better, more unified solution:

```
$userFixtures = $I->getFixture('user');
$user = $userFixtures['basic'];
$userPassword = 'something';
```

Now that we have some basic information about the user, we can try to grab its ID and check if its authentication works altogether:

```
$I->amGoingTo('authenticate to search for my own user');
$I->amHttpAuthenticated($user['username'], $userPassword);
$I->sendGET('users/search/'.$user['username']);
```

The first step is to prepare the request, which is composed of the Authorization header and the actual request. We don't need to explicitly generate the Authorization header, as we have an abstraction over it provided by amHttpAuthenticated(), which would do that for us.

The header is then sent alongside the GET request over our endpoint; note how the URL omits the /v1/ part that we would normally use to prefix the API:

```
$I->seeResponseCodeIs(200);
$I->seeResponseIsJson();
$I->seeResponseContains($user['username']);
$I->seeResponseContains('password');
$I->seeResponseContains('id');
```

Once we've sent the request, we can start analyzing the response and do various assertions on it:

```
$userId = $I->grabDataFromJsonResponse('id');
```

Finally, we grab the user ID from the response, so we can reuse it afterwards.

The next step is about fetching the user's own information knowing their ID, which looks particularly straightforward to implement:

```
$I->amGoingTo('ensure I can fetch my own information while being
  authenticated');
$I->amHttpAuthenticated($user['username'], $userPassword);
$I->sendGET('users/'.$userId);
```

```
$I->seeResponseCodeIs(200);
$I->seeResponseIsJson();
$I->seeResponseContains($user['username']);
$I->seeResponseContains('password');
$I->seeResponseContains('id');
```

As the last step, we have kept the tests on updating the password and ensuring that the new password works as expected:

```
$I->amGoingTo('update my own password');
$I->amHttpAuthenticated($user['username'], $userPassword);
$newPassword = 'something else';
$I->sendPUT(
    'users/' . $userId,
    ['password' => $newPassword, 'authkey' => 'updated']
);
$I->seeResponseIsJson();
$I->seeResponseContains('true');
$I->seeResponseCodeIs(200);

$I->amGoingTo('check my new password works');
$I->amHttpAuthenticated($user['username'], $newPassword);
$I->sendHEAD('users/'.$userId);
$I->seeResponseIsJson();
$I->seeResponseContains($user['username']);
$I->seeResponseCodeIs(200);
```

 Please note that due to the length of the tests, we will be keeping them all in one file as it won't affect their legibility, but you can clearly split them in more CEST files to aggregate them in a more concise and logical way.

This should be all you really need to know. We can check that none of the tests will pass at this point, and at the end of the chapter, we will ensure that all of them are finally passing.

 Also note that it's not necessary to call amHttpAuthenticated() to send the authentication header every time as it will be cached after the first call in the CEPT file, and should only be required when the header needs to be updated.

Now that we have seen how easy it is to write a functional test, I can leave the creation of additional tests to you. If you want, you can start by checking that the rest of the interfaces have not been exposed, such as the ability to request the list of all users and retrieve or change their passwords.

In the following section of this chapter, we are going to focus on the implementation side of the things by looking at some new, shiny features provided by Yii 2.

Creating a RESTful web service with Yii 2

It's important to remember that a REST web service is by definition a stateless service, this will imply some requirements in the way we will test things and deal with the information we need to POST or GET.

The big step forward that Yii made with version 2 can be seen in the built-in REST classes that provide an immediate solution once provided by third-party implementations.

This means we'll have to introduce several changes to what we've achieved so far; the REST part of the application will be developed as a separate module, which will give us the ability to extend it and contain its logic. Because of this, the routes will be rearranged appropriately as well.

Before seeing what the Yii REST functionality is capable of doing, we'll need to first have a quick look at modules in Yii, which we will use to develop our API to be tested.

Writing modular code in Yii

If you've never used modules since you've started working with Yii, well, I think it's time to do so. Right now, modules are really easy and straightforward to use, and they will help you keep your code architecturally well organized and separated from the other components of your application.

Modules are self-contained software units that contain models, views and controllers, and other software components, and the end user will be able to access the controller once it is installed in the main application. For this reason, modules are considered mini-applications, only difference being that they cannot live on their own. As an example, a forum or an administrative area can be developed as modules.

Modules can also be composed of submodules; a forum might have an admin submodule that contains all the logic and interfaces to moderate and customize the main forum module.

Modules can be quite complex in their structure; I would always strongly suggest an architectural analysis before deciding to keep everything under the same module, in the same way as you need to question your choices if you were to keep all the code in the same controller. Always try to keep in mind that you should be able to understand your code in one year's time.

Creating a module with Gii

Developing the REST interface using Yii modules is the easiest way to achieve versioning of the API. This way, we can easily switch and make an improved version of the API while still continuing to support the old version with minimal maintenance, until full deprecation.

So we will start with the creation of the module, using the web interface to the code generator called Gii. In case you skipped a few pages, the configuration for that is available in *Chapter 4, Isolated Component Testing with PHPUnit*, where you saw how to create a model with it.

Now, we will see how to create a module and what this will mean in terms of generated code.

So, head over to the Gii application, which in my case is `http://basic.yii2.sandbox/gii` and log in, if you are configured to do so and click on the **Module Generator** button.

The only two fields we have to fill in are these:

- **Module Class**: This represents the main name-spaced class name of the module, which will be set to `app\modules\v1\Module`.
- **Module ID**: This will be (automatically) set to `v1`.

Have a look at the following screenshot:

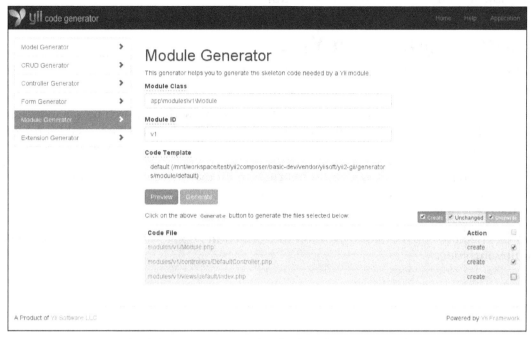

Module generator page within the Gii code generation tool

You can avoid creating the view by deselecting the related checkbox, as we're not going to need one. We're going to make more changes to what has been generated.

Click on the **Generate** button, once ready.

If your application will end up being more complex than what we have here, you still have a few options.

You can simply adjust the routes for the module, as explained in the documentation at `http://www.yiiframework.com/doc-2.0/ guide-runtime-routing.html#adding-rules-dynamically`.

Otherwise, you can create a module within a module (for example, a container module called `api` which will contain the various versions as modules such as `v1`, `v2`, and so on). Just remember to namespace it correctly when creating it. This is usually the solution I'd recommend from the code organization point of view.

The next step is to configure the module in order to be able to use it, and then we will see how to transform it into a REST module.

Using modules in Yii 2

Now that we have our basic code for our module ready, we need to see how we can use it.

Ideally, the created module can be used straight away without much hassle, which is quite helpful in an environment where you want to be able to create reusable and, of course, modular code.

The only step that's really needed is instructing Yii that there is a new module, and in return, it will take care of auto-loading and calling our module controller at the right time.

So let's head over to our configuration file located in `/config/web.php` and add the following code:

```
// /config/web.php

$config = [
    // ...
    'modules' => [
        'v1' => [
            'class' => 'app\modules\v1\Module',
        ],
    ],
    // ...
];
```

With this, you're ready to go. In order to convert the newly created module to act as a REST controller, it requires some additional changes, which we will explore immediately.

Converting our controller to be a REST controller

This much anticipated feature of Yii 2 lets you create a REST interface in a clear and easy way.

The REST controller we will inherit from will deal with our models without much configuration needed and even if there was, it's quite straightforward to do and keep in mind.

Our first step is to create `UserController` which will be dealt with the `User` model.

Let's start by defining the namespace and the basic classes we're going to use in our new controller:

```
// /modules/v1/controllers/UserController.php

namespace app\modules\v1\controllers;

use app\models\User;
use yii\rest\ActiveController;
```

As we can clearly see, we're going to use the `User` model and on top of it the REST `ActiveController`. This controller is where the magic happens, and we're going to illustrate what it is all about in a moment.

Now, let's implement the actual class:

```
// /modules/v1/controllers/UserController.php

class UserController extends ActiveController
{
    public $modelClass = 'app\models\User';
}
```

The only thing needed at this point is just the definition of the model class that the REST controller is going to manage and that's it.

`yii\rest\ActiveController` is the controller that will deal with Active Records models, such as our `User` model. If you were to manage custom classes (non active records) that do not connect to a database or do connect to a custom data source (for instance, an online service), you can use the class that `ActiveController` is inheriting from, which is `yii\rest\Controller`.

The beauty of `ActiveController` is that it provides already implemented actions that are available immediately, which are:

- `index`, which is accessed via GET or HEAD and returns the list of the models and their (database-bound) attributes
- `view`, which is accessed via GET and HEAD and returns the details of a single model
- `create`, which can be accessed only via POST and lets you create a new model
- `update`, which is accessed via PUT or PATCH and does what it says on the tin
- `delete`, which is used to delete a model and can be invoked using DELETE
- `OPTIONS`, which, lastly, you can invoke to see all the allowed HTTP methods

In the actions that you'll be able to implement yourself, you will be dealing with the raw models, which are rendered by default in XML and JSON (depending on the `Accept` header that was sent along with the request).

We know we'll need to modify the list of exposed endpoints, and we'll see how to do it in a moment.

Before getting there, there are a few other bits that need to be addressed first, in particular the access credentials, as we don't want anybody to access our endpoints without being authenticated.

Adding the access check and security layer

You might already have asked yourself how to prevent non-authenticated users from using certain endpoints of your application. For instance, we might want to give a client access to the user endpoint only if it's authenticated and authorized.

The authorization and authentication happen at two different phases.

Authorization is done at controller level by simply overriding the `checkAccess()` method and performing the right checks, which might involve establishing if the user has been authenticated and if he/she is active, in case this flag exists in the user model.

In our case, we can simply add the following method to our controller:

```
// /modules/v1/controllers/UserController.php

public function checkAccess($action, $model = null, $params = [])
{
    if (\Yii::$app->user->isGuest) {
        throw new UnauthorizedHttpException;
    }
}
```

This means that if the user is a guest, we raise a `401` response.

Yii will automatically call the method on each request as we can see in the `actions()` method in its parent class, which is `\yii\rest\ActiveController`:

```
class ActiveController extends Controller
{
    // ...

    public function actions()
    {
```

```
        return [
            'index' => [
                'class' => 'yii\rest\IndexAction',
                'modelClass' => $this->modelClass,
                'checkAccess' => [$this, 'checkAccess'],
            ],
            // ...
        ];
    }

    // ...
}
```

Instead, the authentication is done in a completely different way and varies depending on the implementation and level of security you want to implement in the application.

As far as it goes, in case you haven't touched the argument in depth, you have different possibilities, which are:

- **HTTP Basic Auth**: This is basically the same that you would have by using htpasswd and configuring Apache accordingly and is the simplest one available, but needs the username and password to be sent in a header with every request. This requires the communication to work over HTTPS for obvious reasons.

- **Query parameter**: Here, the client is already possessing an access token, which will be sent to the server as a query parameter as https://server. com/users?access-token=xxxxxxx, which is quite handy if you don't have the ability to send additional tokens with the request.

There are some other ways that use a combination of different techniques and/ or asymmetric and symmetric encryption or different types of handshakes to authenticate a client. One of the most well-known, although potentially complex, is **OAuth 2**, which has different implementations as it's considered more of a framework than a well-defined protocol. Most of the well-known social websites such as Google, Twitter, Facebook, and so on implement it. Its Wikipedia page, available at http://en.wikipedia.org/wiki/OAuth, provides some good links and references to help you explore it further.

As encryption and authentication protocols are outside the scope of this book, I've decided to use the simplest solution, which will anyway give us enough hints on where to put our hands, should we want to implement something more robust or complex.

Building the authentication layer

As Yii uses sessions by default, which will violate the stateless constraints of a RESTful server according to the fielding dissertation (http://www.ics.uci.edu/~fielding/pubs/dissertation/rest_arch_style.htm#sec_5_1_3), we will want to disable the session in the module's init() method:

```
// /modules/v1/Module.php

public function init()
{
    parent::init();
    // custom initialization code goes here
    // disable the user session
    \Yii::$app->user->enableSession = false;
}
```

In Yii the actual authentication is then done via the available authenticator behavior.

Yii provides four different authenticators which are:

- HttpBasicAuth: This is used for HTTP Basic Auth, which we will use here
- QueryParamAuth: This is used for query parameter authentication
- HttpBearerAuth: This is used for OAuth and similar methods
- CompositeAuth: This is a way to use multiple cascading authentication methods

Again open our UserController and let's define the one we want to use:

```
// /modules/v1/controllers/UserController.php

public function behaviors()
{
    $behaviors = parent::behaviors();

    $behaviors['authenticator'] = [
        'class' => HttpBasicAuth::className(),
    ];

    return $behaviors;
}
```

If you were to run the tests against this implementation, you will have problems making them pass; the default implementation will use findIdentityByAccessToken() and use the $username part of the header as an access token. So, there's no real password check.

HTTP Basic Auth defines that, together with your request, you will also have to send an `Authorization` header containing `'Basic '.base64($username.':'.$password);`.

As explained in the documentation of the `HttpBasicAuth` class at `https://github.com/yiisoft/yii2/blob/master/framework/filters/auth/HttpBasicAuth.php#L55`, you need to override the `$auth` attribute in order to perform the password authentication in the way that you want.

As you saw, `findIdentityByAccessToken()` is not a method we're going to need, and we have the unit tests that clearly state that. The best way to address this is by adding our authenticator method straight in the definition of the behavior in the following way:

```
// modules/v1/controllers/UserController.php

public function behaviors()
{
    $behaviors = parent::behaviors();

    $behaviors['authenticator'] = [
        'class' => HttpBasicAuth::className(),
        'auth' => function ($username, $password) {
                /** @var User $user */
                $user = User::findByUsername($username);
                if ($user && $user->validatePassword($password)) {
                    return $user;
                }
            }
    ];

    return $behaviors;
}
```

As explained in the documentation, the `auth` attribute should be a function that expects `$username` and `$password` as actual parameters, and returns the user identity if the authentication is verified.

With this last method, implementation of our authentication and authorization scheme should be complete.

Modifying the existing actions

Now that we've restricted access to any other user, we need to re-implement the view and update actions, in order to allow only the currently logged in user to view just his/her details and allow him to update only the password. If you have already started implementing the actions, this won't be enough as the parent class, `yii\rest\Controller`, already implements all the default actions, so we need to redefine their configuration, which happens to be set within the `actions()` method:

```
public function actions()
{
    $actions = parent::actions();
    unset($actions['view'], $actions['update']);
    return $actions;
}
```

Once we unset the two actions, our own overridden methods will be picked up automatically without much else to do:

```
public function actionView($id)
{
    if ($id == Yii::$app->user->getId()) {
        return User::findOne($id);
    }
    throw new ForbiddenHttpException;
}
```

The view action just adds a check on the ID of the user and returns a 403 error, while the update action can be something along the lines of the following code:

```
public function actionUpdate($id)
{
    if (! Yii::$app->request->isPut) {
        return new HttpRequestMethodException();
    }

    /** @var User $user */
    $user = User::findIdentity($id);

    if (Yii::$app->request->post('password') !== null) {
        $user->setPassword(Yii::$app->request->post('password'));
    }

    return $user->save();
}
```

In the update, we only allow changing of the password, after which we return the value of the save method. We could have returned a more comprehensive status, but for our cause, this is good enough.

 We won't actually need to add the check if the request is not a PUT, as the current internal implementation restricts it by default. We'll see in *Chapter 8, Analyzing Testing Information*, how this will be fixed, using the coverage report information.

Adding a new endpoint with parameters

With all we have done, if we try to run the tests on UserAPICept, we will see that it will fail immediately at the first sendGET('user/search') command.

Implementing the new actionSearch() method won't be a problem, and it can be implemented in the following way:

```
public function actionSearch($username)
{
    /** @var User $user */
    $user = User::findByUsername($username);
    if ($user && $user->id === Yii::$app->user->getId()) {
        return $user;
    }
    throw new ForbiddenHttpException;
}
```

What is important to note is how we will customize the routes to add this new action in a "compliant" way.

Switch to the configuration file located at config/web.php and let's start by adding the search action to the list of allowed methods:

```
'only' => ['view', 'update', 'search', 'options']
```

The UrlRule class that is used to create routes exposes some variables that you can configure, either to extend or entirely re-define the patterns and the structure of the tokens. The first are extraPatterns and patterns respectively. Tokens can be used in the patterns and represent the parameters passed to the action.

In Yii terminology, a pattern is a tuple composed of allowed HTTP method(s), the actual structure of the resource to identify, and the corresponding action to be called. The following is an example of this:

```
'GET search/{username}' => 'search'
```

A token is one or more parameters that can be as complex as a regular expression. In the preceding example, {username} is a token and can be defined as shown in the following code:

```
'{username}' => '<username:\\w+>'
```

Our final list of rules will end up looking like the following code:

```php
// config/web.php

'rules' => [
    [
        'class' => 'yii\rest\UrlRule',
        'controller' => 'v1/user',
        'tokens' => [
            '{id}' => '<id:\\d[\\d,]*>',
            '{username}' => '<username:\\w+>'
        ],
        'extraPatterns' => [
            'GET search/{username}' => 'search',
        ],
        'only' => ['view', 'update', 'search', 'options']
    ],
    '/' => 'site/index',
    '<action:\w+>' => 'site/<action>',
    '<controller:\w+>/<id:\d+>' => '<controller>/view',
    '<controller:\w+>/<action:\w+>/<id:\d+>' => '<controller>
      /<action>',
    '<controller:\w+>/<action:\w+>' => '<controller>/<action>',
]
```

The first thing to note is that we had to re-define all the tokens rather than adding them as we are doing with extraPatterns.

In the list of rules, we have defined the REST interface rules before any other as rules are read top to bottom, and the first one that is found matching will be captured. This means that specific rules must stay at the top, while generic catch-all rules are at the bottom.

The preceding configuration will be fed to urlManager, as explained in the official guide at http://www.yiiframework.com/doc-2.0/guide-runtime-routing. html#using-pretty-urls:

```php
'urlManager' => [
    'enablePrettyUrl' => true,
    'showScriptName' => false,
```

```
    'enableStrictParsing' => true,
    'rules' => [ ... ]
]
```

Now we can check that the tests are passing using the following command:

```
../vendor/bin/codecept run functional UserAPICept.php
Codeception PHP Testing Framework v2.0.8
Powered by PHPUnit 4.5-ge3692ba by Sebastian Bergmann and contributors.


Functional Tests (1) --------------------------------------------------
Trying to test the user REST API (UserAPICept)                      Ok
-----------------------------------------------------------------------



Time: 9.8 seconds, Memory: 14.50Mb


OK (1 test, 18 assertions)
```

Summary

In this chapter, you saw many things such as how to write basic functional tests, how to test a REST interface, and the implementation side of things. Given the amount of knowledge condensed here, it might be useful for you to revisit the chapter later on and give yourself enough time to experiment on the single features in more detail and adapt them to your likings.

In the next chapter, you're going to see how to create acceptance tests for your interfaces that will overcome some of the limitations of working with PHPBrowser.

7
Having Fun Doing Browser Testing

We have finally arrived at the last stage of testing: **acceptance testing**. This is the topmost way of testing your application with Codeception in Yii.

As we saw in the initial chapters , functional and acceptance tests are quite similar in form and implementation, so you won't see anything particularly new in this chapter.

It is important to grasp the nature of the tests that we are going to create. We can recall from *Chapter 6*, *Testing the API – PHPBrowser to the Rescue*, that functional tests are used to ensure the technical correctness of what we've built from a higher standpoint than unit tests. Whereas acceptance tests are the best way of ensuring that the acceptance criteria that were defined at the very beginning are still standing after everything is implemented and put together.

In this chapter, we are going to review the existing tests, install and configure **Selenium,** and then implement a small feature that will tie everything together with the work that has already been done.

In this chapter, we will discuss two main topics:

- Introducing Selenium WebDriver
- Creating acceptance tests

Introducing Selenium WebDriver

Yii is shipped with some acceptance tests. They cover the same elements as the functional tests that we've already seen. The only difference between these two tests is technical, and by looking at the configuration you can see that they've been configured to run with PHPBrowser. This setup may be good enough for you, or it may even be better because PHPBrowser runs faster than the available acceptance testing suites.

Setting aside PHPBrowser, which we've covered in *Chapter 6, Testing the API – PHPBrowser to the Rescue*, Codeception can be used with other testing suites, which can perform more realistic frontend tests, including the JavaScript interaction.

Two of the choices you can have are Selenium WebDriver and PhantomJS. We won't touch PhantomJS, and it should be sufficient to know that it is a headless browser testing suite, which uses the WebDriver interface definition.

Selenium WebDriver is also known as Selenium 2.0 + WebDriver. Together with Cucumber, it is probably the most well-known frontend testing tool available. Their use has been improved by some big companies, such as Google. They are stable and have lots of features.

This is a somewhat natural evolution of Selenium 1.0, which had limitations, such as using JavaScript for interacting with web pages. For this reason, it was running on the JavaScript sandbox. This meant that, in order to get around the same-origin policy, it had to run in conjunction with a Selenium RC server, which had some issues with the browser setup.

Now the Selenium Server has replaced the RC, while remaining retro-compatible and supporting WebDriver natively.

WebDriver uses a native implementation of the browser to interact with it. This means that it might not always be available for a specific combination of language / device. However, it provides the best flexibility for controlling a page without needing emulation.

Codeception uses a PHP implementation called php-webdriver, which was developed by Facebook; its source code and issue tracker can be found at `https:// github.com/facebook/php-webdriver`.

In its simplest implementation and configuration, the Selenium Server just listens for calls as a service on a specific machine, and fires up the browser on the request to perform the tests.

So, as a first step, we need to install the Selenium Server, run it, configure it in Codeception, adjust the already existing tests such that they work with it, and then add the new tests to it.

Installing and running Selenium Server

From version 1.7 onwards, Codeception includes the out-of-the-box php-webdriver library.

As reported in the documentation, which can be found either from Codeception (`http://codeception.com/11-20-2013/webdriver-tests-with-codeception.html`) or from the official page of Selenium (`http://docs.seleniumhq.org/docs/03_webdriver.jsp`), you need to download the server binary and then run it on the machine from, which you intend to run your browser.

Head to `http://www.seleniumhq.org/download/` and download the latest version of the software. In my case, it would be `selenium-server-standalone-2.44.0.jar`.

Where you save it doesn't matter because once it starts, its server will be listening to any network interface:

```
$ java -jar selenium-server-standalone-2.44.0.jar
22:03:31.892 INFO - Launching a standalone server
22:03:31.980 INFO - Java: Oracle Corporation 24.65-b04
22:03:31.980 INFO - OS: Linux 3.17.1 amd64
22:03:32.002 INFO - v2.44.0, with Core v2.44.0. Built from revision 76d78cf
...
```

Configuring Yii to work with Selenium

In order to have Codeception automatically pick up and use WebDriver, we need to adjust our acceptance suite configuration:

```
# tests/codeception/acceptance.suite.yml
class_name: AcceptanceTester
modules:
    enabled:
        - WebDriver
    config:
        WebDriver:
            url: 'http://basic-dev.yii2.sandbox'
            browser: firefox
            host: 192.168.56.1
            restart: true
            window_size: 1024x768
```

This is a straightforward process. We need to replace the PHPBrowser module with WebDriver and configure it.

- `url` (required): This is the hostname used to connect to your application to perform the tests.

- `browser` (required): This will specify the browser that you want to use. Some other drivers are also available for mobile phones (Android and iOS), and more information about these can be obtained from the online Selenium documentation, available at `http://docs.seleniumhq.org/docs/03_webdriver.jsp#selenium-webdriver-s-drivers`.

- `host`: This key specifies the machine that will run the Selenium Server. By default, it will connect to your localhost. For example, I am using the VirtualBox host machine IP address. You can also specify the port and by default, it will use `4444`.

- `restart`: This tells WebDriver to reset a session when a test is performed. This is particularly handy if you don't want a state to be carried over from one test to another. For instance, you can use this when you need to (re)set the cookies to test the auto login functionality.

- `window_size`: This just specifies the size of the window.

There are other options, some of which will be quite handy for testing with multiple browsers. In particular, you have the ability to set the desired capabilities for Selenium 2.0, such as being able to pass a specific profile for the browser (quite handy when performing regression testing) and so on. More information about the WebDriver module, albeit not as much as I'd love to see, can be found on the Codeception documentation page at `http://codeception.com/docs/modules/WebDriver`.

Implementing WebDriver-led tests

Before we start implementing the interface that will hook into the API, which we implemented in *Chapter 6, Testing the API – PHPBrowser to the Rescue*, it would be quite useful to look at the existing acceptance tests and see if there's anything new that we need to take into consideration.

You will find four tests: `HomeCept`, `AboutCept`, `LoginCept`, and `ContactCept`.

As stated previously, the syntax is not unusual, and we can see that the level of knowledge of the underlying structure is more limited than the functional tests that we've covered.

The important thing that we need to stress on once again is that all the actions that our `AcceptanceTester` can perform on the page, such as `click()`, `fillField()`, and the assertions that it can perform, such as `see()`, `seeLink()` and so on, accept a so-called Locator as one of its actual parameters.

The Locator parameter can be either a string or an array.

When passed as a string or a **fuzzy locator,** as it is called in the Codeception terminology, it tries to guess what you're looking for by formally going through a series of steps. If you write `click('foo')`, then it will do the following:

1. It tries to find the element with the ID `#foo`.

2. It tries to find the class `.foo`.

3. Then, it interprets it as an XPath expression.

4. Finally, it will throw an `ElementNotFound` exception.

You can be more prescriptive when using the array notation or a **strict locator.**

*   `['id' => 'foo']` matches `<div id="foo">`

*   `['name' => 'foo']` matches `<div name="foo">`

*   `['css' => 'input[type=input][value=foo]']` matches `<input type="input" value="foo">`

*   `['xpath' => "//input[@type='submit'][contains(@value, 'foo')]"]` matches `<input type="submit" value="foobar">`

*   `['link' => 'Click here']` matches `<a href="google.com">Click here</a>`

*   `['class' => 'foo']` matches `<div class="foo">`

The preceding examples have been taken from the Codeception documentation, which can be found at `http://codeception.com/docs/modules/WebDriver`.

This explains clearly how to interact with the webpage. Now, the other important bit can be found in the already existing tests, such as `LoginCept` and `ContactCept`. Here, right before asserting the presence of the validation errors, we have the following condition-led statement:

```
if (method_exists($I, 'wait')) {
    $I->wait(3); // only for selenium
}
```

Selenium introduces two types of wait: an implicit one and an explicit one. These cause the information to be fetched from the server, and then this information is interpreted and rendered.

The implicit wait can be configured in the `acceptance.suite.yml` file, and it silently tells Selenium to poll for *X* seconds if the element it's looking for is not immediately available. By default, no implicit wait is set.

The explicit wait is similar to the preceding code snippet. Doing a simple `$I->wait(X)` triggers a `sleep()`, and allows the browser to perform the required operation. For example, it would help the browser in completing animations or finishing fetching and manipulating the server-side data.

There are other ways in which you can wait for something, and some of these ways can be a little more proactive, such as `waitForElement()`, `waitForElementChange()`, `waitForElementVisible()` and `waitForElementNotVisible()`. All these methods take a locator, using the aforementioned format, and a timeout in seconds as parameters. We will see how we can use these later on.

There are other methods provided by the WebDriver Codeception module that you can use, along with the ability to debug your tests, in case something doesn't go as you want.

Now, let's try to run the available tests and see them pass:

```
$ ../vendor/bin/codecept run acceptance
Codeception PHP Testing Framework v2.0.9
Powered by PHPUnit 4.6-dev by Sebastian Bergmann and contributors.


Acceptance Tests (5) --------------------------------------------------
----------
Trying to ensure that about works (AboutCept) Ok
Trying to ensure that contact works (ContactCept) Ok
Trying to ensure that home page works (HomeCept) Ok
Trying to ensure that login works (LoginCept) Ok
-------------------------------------------------------------


Time: 38.54 seconds, Memory: 13.00Mb


OK (4 tests, 23 assertions)
```

Depending on which machine you'll be using for running these tests, their speed will change sensibly, although it will never be as fast as it's when performing unit tests, mostly because the whole browser stack has to be started for running these tests.

You will briefly see the browser opening and closing several times while performing the tests. Everything should look good at the end, and if it doesn't, then look into the `tests/codeception/_output/` folder. Here, you will find a markup and a screenshot of the page taken at the time of the failure. This debugging behavior is also found in the functional tests while using PHPBrowser.

Creating acceptance tests

Now that we have seen how the acceptance tests that use Selenium WebDriver are structured, we can start integrating the work done in the previous chapter and begin adding the tests we want.

For these kinds of tests, where normally the definition of the markup is left to whoever implements the layout, you would need to define the functionality of your interface, implement the tests, and then implement the markup and add the JavaScript functionality, if needed. After you've performed these, you will add the specifics of the DOM interaction.

Knowing how many developers leave the frontend functionality definition for the very end, working "tests first" will force you to change your way of working, anticipating with as much detail as needed what lies ahead and discovering immediately any critical aspects of the design.

We will try to implement something that is simple enough to get you started with from scratch and then you can improve upon or extend it later. We know that the HTTP Basic Auth, which we have used, does not permit a stateful login. Therefore, we will have to keep some sort of a session object in JavaScript to simulate it. How this is going to work can be taken from the tests that we have written for the User API. This is practical documentation at its best.

So, our scenario can be described as follows:

```
I WANT TO TEST MODAL LOGIN

I am on homepage
I see link 'Login'
I don't see link 'Logout' # i.e. I'm not logged
I am going to 'test the login with empty credentials'
```

```
.I click 'Login'
I wait for modal to be visible
I submit form with empty credentials
I see 'Error'

I am going to 'test the login with wrong credentials'
I submit form with wrong credentials
I see 'Error'

I am going to 'test the login with valid credentials'
I submit form with valid credentials
I don't see the modal anymore
I see link 'Logout'
I don't see link 'Login'

I am going to 'test logout'
I click 'Logout'
I don't see link 'Logout'
I see link 'Login'
```

The preceding syntax has been taken explicitly from the generated text version of our tests.

Implementing the modal window

The work of implementing the modal window will be made easy by Bootstrap, which is a default framework bundled with the basic app.

The modal window is composed by an almost pre-determined markup and an additional JS, which provides the interaction part, thereby hooking it to the rest of the interface. I hope that the simplicity of its implementation will let you focus on the aim that lies behind it.

The following code has deliberately been taken from the Bootstrap documentation, which can be found at http://getbootstrap.com/javascript/#modals. Since the modal window can be opened from any part of the website without going to the login page, we will have to add it to the overall layout template:

```
<!-- views/layouts/main.ph -->
</footer>

<div class="modal fade" id="myModal" tabindex="-1"
  role="dialog" aria-labelledby="myModalLabel" aria-
  hidden="true">
    <div class="modal-dialog">
```

```
            <div class="modal-content">
                <div class="modal-header">
                    <button type="button" class="close" data-
                        dismiss="modal"><span aria-hidden="true">
                        &times;</span><span class="sr-only">
                        Close</span></button>
                    <h4 class="modal-title">Login</h4>
                </div>
                <div class="modal-body">
                    <?= $this->render('/site/login-modal.php',
                        ['model' => Yii::$app->controller-
                        >loginForm]); ?>
                </div>
            </div>
        </div>
    </div>

<?php $this->endBody() ?>
<!-- ... -->
```

As you can see, we have moved the modal form to a separate template, which will receive the model of the form as a variable, keeping everything self-contained and organized. Please note from where the model takes its value. We're going to discuss it while implementing the controller.

The login-modal.php template is just a rip-off of the original login.php template, which can be found in the same directory without H1 in the title and the "remember me" checkbox. We just need to add a placeholder to show the error that is coming from the API. This is done to inform and debug it.

```
<!-- views/site/login-modal.php
<!-- ... -->
<div class="alert alert-danger alert-dismissible fade in">
    <button type="button" class="close" data-dismiss="alert"><span
        aria-hidden="true">x</span><span class="sr-only">
        Close</span></button>
    <p class="error"></p>
</div>
<!-- ... -->
```

We can place this snippet right after the first paragraph of the copied markup.

Making the server side work

As we have said before, we want the modal window to be available everywhere. We are going to accomplish this by saving a publicly accessible property in the `SiteController`, so that we can retrieve it from the view. Remember that if you're coming from Yii 1, then views are now separate objects and not a part of the controller.

Let's use the `init()` method to do so:

```php
// controllers/SiteController.php

public $loginForm = null;

public function init()
{
    $this->loginForm = new LoginForm();
}
```

Once this is done, we can load our page without errors.

In the next step, we will add the interaction to JavaScript.

Adding the JavaScript interaction

We will cover a couple of things in this section. We will discuss the basic functional interaction with the modal, the interaction with the form, and then learn how to close everything with the corner cases and error scenarios.

The interaction with the modal will be achieved by reusing the already existing login button, which is at the top right side of the menu. We will disable it, but remember that it will provide a fallback compatibility in case something goes wrong.

The basic open-and-close of the modal window is provided out-of-the-box. We will only trigger it when required, for example upon authentication success.

Let's add the first basic skeleton for the JS module:

```javascript
// web/js/main.js

var YII = YII || {};
```

For this part of our application, we will need the module pattern for creating a self-contained application.

```javascript
YII.main = (function ($) {
    'use strict';
```

Let's start by caching all the jQuery elements that we are going to need along the way:

```
var $navbar = $('.navbar-nav.nav'),
    $modal = $('#myModal'),
    $modalBody = $modal.find('.modal-body'),
    $modalAlertBox = $modal.find('.alert').hide(),
    $modalError = $modalAlertBox.find('.error'),
    $CTALogin = $navbar.find('.login'),
```

Once we have logged in, we will swap the link with a "fake" logout button:

```
    $CTALogout = $('<li class="logout"><a href="#">
      Logout</a></li>'),
```

We will need some data fields for holding our login information and creating some sort of a session:

```
    authorization = null,
    username = null,
    userID = null;
```

Now comes the main part of our script, in which we will initialize our event listeners to the click and submit actions:

```
/**
 * initialise all the events in the page.
 */
(function init() {
    $navbar.append($CTALogout);
    $CTALogout.hide();
```

Let's start by appending and hiding our logout button; we will show it only when the login succeeds, and define the click action it should have:

```
    $navbar.on('click', '.logout a', function (e) {
        e.preventDefault();

        // unset the user info
        authorization = null;
        username = null;
        userID = null;

        // restore the login CTA
        $CTALogout.hide();
        $CTALogin.show();
    });
```

We need to disable the click event for the login button. Otherwise, we will be taken to the login page, instead of opening the modal:

```
$navbar.on('click', '.login a', function (e) {
    e.preventDefault();
});
```

The modal triggering event is done automatically by modifying the markup of the login button. So, navigate to `views/layouts/main.php` and then adjust it as follows:

```
'label' => 'Login',
'url' => ['/site/login'],
'options' => [
    'data-toggle'=>'modal',
    'data-target'=> '#myModal',
    'class' => 'login'
]
```

Next, we will deal with the form submission:

```
$modalBody.on('submit', '#login-form', function (e) {
    e.preventDefault();
```

After disabling the default submit event, we will need to capture the username and the password, and then save it for future use:

```
username = this['loginform-username'].value;
// we don't care to store the password... sorta
authorization = btoa(username + ':' + this['loginform-
    password'].value);
```

The `authorization` variable will hold our authorization header that is ready for dispatch:

```
$.ajax(
    {
        method: 'GET',
        url: '/v1/users/search/' + username,
        dataType: 'json',
        async: false,
        beforeSend: authorize,
        complete: function (xhr, status) {

            if (status === 'success') {
                // save the user ID
                userID = xhr.responseJSON.id;
                // set the logout button
```

```
                              $CTALogin.hide();
                              $CTALogout.show();
                              // clear the status errors
                              $modalError.html('');
                              $modalAlertBox.hide();
                              // close the modal window
                              $modal.modal('hide');
                          }
                          else {
                              // display the error
                              $modalError.html('<strong>Error
                                </strong>: ' + xhr.statusText);
                              $modalAlertBox.show();
                          }
                      }
                  }
              );
          });
      })();
  })(jQuery);
```

This code is simple enough. In case of success, we save the user ID for subsequent
calls, we hide the login button and display the logout one, clear the error message,
and hide the modal window. Otherwise, we just display the error message.

The `beforesend` option will be initialized by the `authorize` function, which is
defined as follows:

```
/**
 * modifies the XHR object to include the authorization
   headers.
 *
 * @param {jqXHR} xhr the jQuery XHR object, is automatically
   passed at call time
 */
function authorize(xhr) {
    xhr.setRequestHeader('Authorization', 'Basic ' +
      authorization);
}
```

After doing this, we won't need anything else to interact with the page. So, let's put
everything together.

Tying everything together

At this point, we only have to add our JS to the page and then finalize our tests. In order to add our file to the page, we need to know what assets and asset bundles are.

Dealing with Yii 2 assets bundles

Yii 2 has radically changed the way assets are handled. It has introduced the concept of the asset bundle.

Asset bundles are collections of scripts and style sheets that can have a higher degree of configurability as compared to the past.

This basic app already has a basic implementation. So, let's navigate to /assets/ AppAsset.php and see how the content is structured:

```php
<?php // assets/AppAsset.php

namespace app\assets;

use yii\web\AssetBundle;

class AppAsset extends AssetBundle
{
    public $basePath = '@webroot';
    public $baseUrl = '@web';
    public $css = [
        'css/site.css',
    ];
    public $js = [];
    public $depends = [
        'yii\web\YiiAsset',
        'yii\bootstrap\BootstrapAsset',
    ];
}
```

The AppAsset extends from the yii\web\AssetBundle class and it simply defines a series of public properties.

The first two properties, $basePath and $baseUrl, are the most important ones. $basePath defines where the assets are located on a publicly accessible location, while $baseUrl defines how their resource is linked to the web pages, that is, their URL.

This asset, by using these two properties, defines the so called "published asset". In other words, it defines a bundle of assets, which are available at a publicly accessible location.

You can have "external assets", which are comprised of resources from external locations, and "source assets", which are not comprised of resources from publicly available locations. These assets define only a `$sourcePath` property and Yii copies them to the publicly accessible assets folder, and names them accordingly.

Source assets are normally provided by libraries and widgets, and for this reason, we won't be covering them here. Published assets are recommended for incorporating assets into the page or pages by putting them somewhere in the `web/` folder.

In the example earlier, you saw that we defined the asset dependencies, and in our case, it's done with jQuery and Bootstrap. This is exactly why we've used them for developing the main JavaScript module.

Lastly, we need to see how we can use the asset bundle for our markup. This can be done by looking at the top of the template view. For this, navigate to `/views/layouts/main.php`. Here, we can see these two lines:

```
// views/layouts/main.php
use app\assets\AppAsset;
AppAsset::register($this);
```

Remember that the old way of associating any asset with a specific layout, although it's not particularly advisable, hasn't been removed. This works in the same way as it was working in Yii 1, that is, by using `registerCssFile()` and `registerJsFile()`.

Assets have many other options, such as the ability to compress and compile SASS and LESS files, use Bower or NPM assets, and so on. Go to the documentation page, which is currently in a good shape and is quite comprehensive, at `http://www.yiiframework.com/doc-2.0/guide-structure-assets.html`.

For our work, we need to slightly adjust the asset bundle provided by adding the JS file and tweak it where it's going to be added to the page, otherwise we will encounter some problems in running it before the page is parsed. Consider the following code snippet:

```
public $js = [
    'js/main.js',
];
public $jsOptions = [
    'position' => \yii\web\View::POS_END
];
```

Once you've added the preceding lines to the asset bundle, you need to head back to the form template that is included in the modal. This, in fact, will generate some problems because it requires injecting some script into the page in order to make the client-side validation work. This is a major problem; most of the time you will have to override the way `ActiveForms` works, so you should learn how to do it.

```php
// views/site/login-modal.php

<?php $form = ActiveForm::begin([
    'id' => 'login-form',
    'options' => ['class' => 'form-horizontal'],
    'enableClientScript' => false,
    'enableClientValidation' => false,
    'fieldConfig' => [
        'template' => "{label}\n<div class=\"col-lg-
            4\">{input}</div>\n<div class=\"col-lg-
            5\">{error}</div>",
        'labelOptions' => ['class' => 'col-lg-offset-1 col-lg-
            2 control-label'],
    ],
]); ?>
```

The two options shown here will disable both the client-side validation and any additional scripting facility. Disabling only one option won't do the trick.

We can now load the page and no error message will be displayed on the console.

Finalizing the tests

At this point, we just have to convert our scenarios into live code.

Let's start creating the test in the same way as we created unit tests and functional tests:

```
$ ../vendor/bin/codecept generate:cept acceptance LoginModalCept
Test was created in LoginModalCept.php
```

Navigate to the file and let's start by asserting the initial statements: where we are and ensure that we are not logged in:

```php
<?php
// tests/codeception/acceptance/LoginModalCept.php
$I = new AcceptanceTester($scenario);
$I->wantTo('test modal login');

$I->amOnPage(Yii::$app->homeUrl);
```

```
$I->seeLink('Login');
$I->dontSeeLink('Logout');
```

Although this might seem like a simplistic way of determining whether the user is logged in, it serves the purpose. If we find that anything more complex is needed, then we can always add it to the mix later:

```
$I->amGoingTo('test the login with empty credentials');
$I->click('Login');
$I->waitForElementVisible('.modal');
$I->fillField('#loginform-username', '');
$I->fillField('#loginform-password', '');
$I->click('#login-form button');
$I->see('Error', '.alert .error');
```

The most important part of this test is the use of an explicit wait, `waitForElementVisible()`. It does what it says on the tin: waits until the DOM element with class .modal is rendered and visible.

The assertion made at the end does not check for any specific errors. So feel free to add any level of customization here, as I've tried to be as generic as possible.

The same goes for the following test:

```
$I->amGoingTo('test the login with wrong credentials');
$I->fillField('#loginform-username', 'admin');
$I->fillField('#loginform-password', 'wrong password');
$I->click('#login-form button');
$I->see('Error', '.alert .error');
```

This interesting part of the test comes when we're trying to access using valid credentials. In fact, as we've seen in the script we created previously, the modal window will be dismissed and the login button will be replaced by the logout link:

```
$I->amGoingTo('test the login with valid credentials');
$I->fillField('#loginform-username', 'admin');
$I->fillField('#loginform-password', 'admin');
$I->click('#login-form button');
$I->wait(3);
$I->dontSeeElement('.modal');
$I->seeLink('Logout');
$I->dontSeeLink('Login');
```

In order to do this, we need to add another explicit wait for the AJAX call to complete and then the window will disappear. Using `waitForElementNotVisible()` might not do the trick because it involves animation. It also depends on the responsiveness of the system you're testing on because it might not work as expected and fail from time to time. So, `wait()` seems like the simplest solution for the problem. Consider this code snippet:

```
$I->amGoingTo('test logout');
$I->click('Logout');
$I->dontSeeLink('Logout');
$I->seeLink('Login');
```

The last test doesn't need much attention and you should be able to understand it without facing any problems.

Now that we have put together our tests, let's run them:

```
$ ../vendor/bin/codecept run acceptance
Codeception PHP Testing Framework v2.0.9
Powered by PHPUnit 4.6-dev by Sebastian Bergmann and contributors.


Acceptance Tests (6) ---------------------------------------------
Trying to ensure that about works (AboutCept) Ok
Trying to ensure that contact works (ContactCept) Ok
Trying to ensure that home page works (HomeCept) Ok
Trying to ensure that login works (LoginCept) Ok
Trying to test modal login (LoginModalCept) Ok

------------------------------------------------------------------


Time: 47.33 seconds, Memory: 13.00Mb


OK (5 tests, 32 assertions)
```

Testing multiple browsers

Version 1.7 onwards, Codeception also provides a method for testing multiple browsers. This is not particularly difficult, and it can ensure that cross-browser compatibility is achieved.

This is normally done by configuring environments in the `acceptance.suite.yml` file by adding something similar to the following at the bottom of the file:

```
env:
    chrome39:
        modules:
            config:
                WebDriver:
                    browser: chrome
    firefox34:
        # nothing changed
    ie10:
        modules:
            config:
                WebDriver:
                    host: 192.168.56.102
                    browser: internetexplorer
```

Each key under the `env` variable represents a specific browser you want to run the test on, and this is done by overriding the default configuration that we have already defined.

 Within env, you can override just about any other key that was specified in the YAML configuration files.

You can have several machines, each having different versions of the browsers, with Selenium Server listening on them, so you can also perform retro-compatibility tests when deciding which polyfills to use for the new features introduced recently and also depending on your browser support chart.

In order to trigger the various environments, just append the `--env <environment>` parameter to the `run` command:

```
$ ../vendor/bin/codecept run acceptance --env chrome39 --env firefox34 --env ie10
```

Internet Explorer requires its own driver to be installed on the host machine and a few more steps to be performed to set it up correctly, which is covered in the Selenium documentation, which can be found at `https://code.google.com/p/selenium/wiki/InternetExplorerDriver`.

Understanding Selenium limits

By now, you have probably seen how powerful Selenium is. By using the browser natively, you can finally interact with the website programmatically. This will save a huge portion of time that is normally spent by human beings on doing repetitive tasks. Repetitiveness is only a cause of problems when it comes into the hands of humans, so this is effectively a good thing.

Unfortunately Selenium can't do everything, and if you have already started looking into it and researching its full use and potential, then you might have noticed that there are some limitations of its use.

Clearly any kind of "pixel-perfect" tests are nearly impossible to recreate with Selenium, although some types of tests on designs can be created, specifically for responsive designs. Other frameworks, such as Galen cover this functionality (http://galenframework.com/).

A few words need to be spent on hover effects, as they might be quite difficult to achieve and you may need to use the `moveMouseOver()` method for triggering it.

Summary

We have covered the final aspect of testing in this chapter. We've gone through the provided tests. We have also understood any additional syntax, configured Selenium, run the first batch of tests, and then moved on to implementing and tying the API previously developed into the interface with a modal login feature.

In the next chapter, we are going to learn about a lot of logs and how information can be generated by our tests to better our understanding of testing. We will also see if we've missed anything.

8
Analyzing Testing Information

In the last three chapters, we covered the topic of writing tests at different levels: unit, functional, and acceptance. So far, we have tested the new interface that we created, and we learned to apply all the new methods. This was a relatively easy task, but we don't know how good we did in our testing. There are some specific metrics that we can analyze to generate a direct and immediate report on the quality of the tests. These reports will help us in taking informed decisions regarding the architecture of our code.

Codeception is bundled with most of these report generation tools, and it's quite easy as it's been until now.

In this chapter, we will primarily cover the code coverage metrics, and we'll briefly touch on some other metrics, which can be obtained through various software.

- Improving the quality of your tests
- Improving our code with the aid of additional tools

Improving the quality of your tests

Since the beginning of programming and, in particular, testing, many programmers started questioning themselves on what it means to write good tests, or in other words, how do I know that the test I have written is good? What are the metrics for this?

It's definitely not a question of personal preference or skill.

One of the first methods that was created for analyzing the quality of the tests was called code coverage. From a wider perspective, code coverage measures how much of the code is covered by the tests. There is a correlation between software bugs and the test code coverage, where the software with more code coverage has fewer bugs, although the tests won't remove the possibility of bugs being introduced, for instance, as a manifestation of complex interactions between modules or unexpected inputs and corner cases. This is why you need to be careful when planning and designing your tests, and you need to take into consideration that this won't remove the need for regression and exploratory testing, at least, not entirely.

There are several code coverage criteria that are normally used for the code coverage programs.

- **Line coverage**: This is based on the number of executable lines that were executed.

- **Function and method coverage**: This calculates the number of functions or methods that were executed.

- **Class and trait coverage**: This measures the covered classes and traits when all of their methods are executed.

- **Opcode coverage**: This is similar to line coverage, although a single line might generate more than one opcode. The line coverage considers a line to have been covered as soon as one of its opcodes are executed.

- **Branch coverage**: This measures if each possible combination of Boolean expression in the control structures are being evaluated when the tests are run.

- **Path coverage**: This is also called **Decision-to-Decision (DD)** path, and it considers all the possible execution paths, in terms of its unique sequence of branch execution from the beginning to the end of each method or function.

- **Change Risk Anti-Patterns (C.R.A.P.) Index**: This is based on the cyclomatic complexity and the code coverage of a unit of code. This index can be lowered by refactoring the code or by incrementing the number of tests. Either way, it's primarily used for unit tests.

Since Codeception uses PHP_CodeCoverage, it does not support opcode coverage, branch coverage, and path coverage.

With this in mind, if we go back to our unit tests, we will understand a bit better the structure of our tests and how they are currently working.

Let's start by enabling the code coverage in our unit tests and then looking at their results.

Later, we will look at the functional and acceptance coverage reports, and then explore some other interesting information, which we can extract from our code.

Enabling code coverage in Codeception

Codeception provides a global and a specific configuration for code coverage. Depending on the structure of your application and the type of test you are going to implement based on your test plan, you can have either a generic configuration in /tests/codeception.yml, or a specific configuration for each suite configuration file, such as /tests/codeception/unit.suite.yml. You can also have both of these configurations. However, in this case, the single suite configuration will override the setting of the global configuration.

We are going to use the global configuration file. So at the end of the file, append the following lines:

```
# tests/codeception.yml

coverage:
    enabled: true
    white_list:
        include:
            - ../models/*
            - ../modules/v1/controllers/*
            - ../controllers/*
            - ../commands/*
            - ../mail/*
    blacklist:
        include:
            - ../assets/*
            - ../build/*
            - ../config/*
            - ../runtime/*
            - ../vendor/*
            - ../views/*
            - ../web/*
            - ../tests/*
```

This should be enough for getting started. The first option enables the code coverage, while the rest of the options tell Codeception and the code coverage program which files to include when writing the report for the white list and the black list. This will ensure that the results aggregate the information that is relevant to us, in other words, what we've written, rather than the framework itself.

We won't need to run the `build` command of Codeception, as there isn't a new module that has to be imported into our tester guys.

If we look at the `help` option for the `run` action of Codeception, then we will notice that it has two main options for generating the reports that we are interested in.

- `--coverage`: This generates the actual coverage report, and it is accompanied by a series of other options for controlling the format and the verbosity of the report
- `--report`: This generates an overall report of the tests that were run

In conjunction with these two options, we will be able to generate the HTML and XML test and coverage reports, depending on the use. In particular, the XML report will be quite handy when we get to *Chapter 9, Eliminating Stress with the Help of Automation*.

> It's important to keep in mind that currently the coverage reports of the acceptance tests are not merged with the reports generated for the functional and unit tests. This is due to the way in which the code coverage is calculated and intercepted. Later, we will see what will be needed for generating the coverage reports for acceptance tests.

Extracting the code coverage information for unit tests

In the Codeception documentation, this is normally referred to as the **local coverage** report and it is applied to both the unit and functional tests. We'll touch upon remote coverage when talking about the coverage for acceptance tests.

We can easily generate the coverage by appending the `--coverage` flag to the command shown here:

```
$ ../vendor/bin/codecept run unit --coverage
```

This will end with an output similar to the following:

```
...
Time: 44.93 seconds, Memory: 39.75Mb


OK (32 tests, 68 assertions)
```

```
Code Coverage Report:
  2015-01-05 21:43:13


 Summary:
  Classes: 25.00% (2/8)
  Methods: 45.00% (18/40)
  Lines:   26.42% (56/212)


\app\models::ContactForm
  Methods:  33.33% ( 1/ 3)    Lines:  80.00% ( 12/ 15)
\app\models::Dog
  Methods: 100.00% ( 2/ 2)    Lines: 100.00% (  3/  3)
\app\models::LoginForm
  Methods: 100.00% ( 4/ 4)    Lines: 100.00% ( 18/ 18)
\app\models::User
  Methods:  84.62% (11/13)    Lines:  79.31% ( 23/ 29)
```

> The execution time you see here is based on a machine with an i7-m620 processor, on which runs the Linux kernel. The coverage increases the time exponentially. On the same machine, running the unit tests takes less than 10 seconds.
>
> There are methods for shortening the execution time. This can be done by using Robo, which is a task runner, and its specific Codeception plugin is robo-paracept. More information can be found in the official Codeception documentation at http://codeception.com/docs/12-ParallelExecution.

This report gives us a succinct and immediate output of the code coverage of our unit tests.

The coverage for classes, methods, and lines (and where the percentage is calculated from), and a slightly detailed breakdown per class can be seen from the summary.

We can see that we succeeded in covering 100 percent of the Dog and LoginForm classes, and we nonetheless achieved a good 84.62 percent of the methods of the User class, but disappointingly, we covered only 33.33 percent of the methods of the ContactForm.

But, what did we miss?

Well, there's only one way to find out, and that is by generating the HTML coverage report.

Generating a detailed coverage report of the unit tests

With the help of the `--coverage-html` option, we can generate a detailed code coverage report. Then, we can inspect it in order to understand what was covered and what was missed:

```
$ ../vendor/bin/codecept run unit --coverage-html
```

This will now end with the following output line:

```
HTML report generated in coverage
```

The report will be saved in the `_output/coverage/` directory, where you will find two files: `dashboard.html` and `index.html`. The first gives you some nice graphs, which are a little more interesting than the coverage report summary printed on the console, but it is mostly used for showing off and it is not useful for understanding what's wrong with the tests. There's, in fact, an open request for suppressing this output on the console (`https://github.com/Codeception/Codeception/issues/1592`).

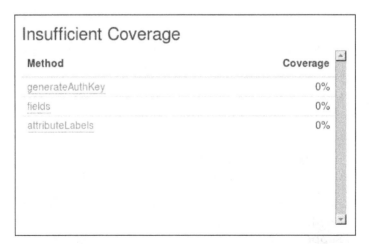

Details of the **Insufficient Coverage** panel on the dashboard

As you can see from the preceding screenshot, the bit that you might be interested in at this level of detail is the **Insufficient Coverage** panel, (currently) sitting at bottom-left of the page.

We will discuss the other panels later.

You will be really interested in the `index.html` file. From there, you can see some of the detailed statistics and you can dig into every single file that has been analyzed, to see what lines the tests have covered and so improve your tests from there.

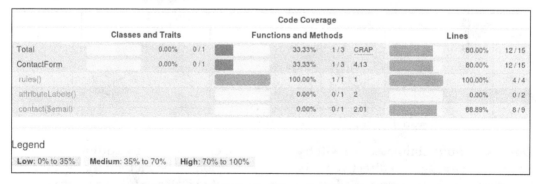

	Code Coverage							
	Lines			Functions and Methods			Classes and Traits	
Total		86.15%	56 / 65		81.82%	18 / 22		50.00%	2 / 4
ContactForm.php		80.00%	12 / 15		33.33%	1 / 3		0.00%	0 / 1
Dog.php		100.00%	3 / 3		100.00%	2 / 2		100.00%	1 / 1
LoginForm.php		100.00%	18 / 18		100.00%	4 / 4		100.00%	1 / 1
User.php		79.31%	23 / 29		84.62%	11 / 13		0.00%	0 / 1

Legend

Low: 0% to 35%   **Medium:** 35% to 70%   **High:** 70% to 100%

Summary of the coverage across all files analyzed

The summary of the coverage shows what's been covered, in some detail. This helped us in discovering immediately what was wrong with our testing, and in our case, one of the tests provided by Yii for `ContactForm` was not covered sufficiently. In the preceding screenshot, we can see that it shows 80 percent coverage of lines, 33.33 percent coverage of the methods, but it does not show anything regarding the classes. This is because, unless you have all the methods covered, you won't have the class marked as covered.

This may not prove be a problem. There are methods that are not a part of our implementation and these can only be tested by using an integration test, and then there are others that can be covered by paying a bit of attention. If we click on the **ContactForm.php** link, then we would see the following:

	Code Coverage							
	Classes and Traits			Functions and Methods			Lines	
Total	0.00%	0 / 1		33.33%	1 / 3	CRAP		80.00%	12 / 15
ContactForm	0.00%	0 / 1		33.33%	1 / 3	4.13		80.00%	12 / 15
rules()				100.00%	1 / 1	1		100.00%	4 / 4
attributeLabels()				0.00%	0 / 1	2		0.00%	0 / 2
contact($email)				0.00%	0 / 1	2.01		88.89%	8 / 9

Legend

Low: 0% to 35%   **Medium:** 35% to 70%   **High:** 70% to 100%

Summary of the coverage of the code in the selected file

Of the two methods that have not been covered, we don't really need to cover the first method, attributeLabels(). Technically, this is because of two reasons: the first reason is that as it is a part of the Yii framework, we assume that it will work; the second reason is that it's a trivial method, and it always returns an internal variable, which can't be controlled in any way.

The other method is the contact() method and it has been covered partially. So, we're going to fix this. It may well be possible that this specific test will get corrected in a future version of the framework. This might be something that you need to look out for.

By clicking on the **contact($email)** link, or by just scrolling to the bottom of the page, we will find our method, and this will show us that all the paths have not been covered.

```
49      public function contact($email)
50      {
51          if ($this->validate()) {
52              Yii::$app->mailer->compose()
53                  ->setTo($email)
54                  ->setFrom([$this->email => $this->name])
55                  ->setSubject($this->subject)
56                  ->setTextBody($this->body)
57                  ->send();
58
59              return true;
60          } else {
61              return false;
62          }
63      }
64  }


Legend

Executed    Not Executed    Dead Code
```

Discovering what needs to be covered with the aid of color coded lines

Our case is quite simple, so we will try to fix these errors either by adding the @codeCoverageIgnore directive to the documentation of the method that we want to exclude, or by adjusting or adding a new test to it in order to reach as close as possible to 100 percent. Remember, this is what we will be aiming for, but this is not necessarily our target.

```
// /tests/codeception/unit/models/ContactFormTest.php

/**
 * @return array customized attribute labels
 * @codeCoverageIgnore
 */
public function attributeLabels()
{
    return [
        'verifyCode' => 'Verification Code',
    ];
}
```

The solution to cover the remaining branch of the `if` statement is to add a test similar to the following:

```
// /tests/codeception/unit/models/ContactFormTest.php

public function testContactReturnsFalseIfModelDoesNotValidate()
{
    $model = $this->getMock(
            'app\models\ContactForm', ['validate']
    );
    $model->expects($this->any())
            ->method('validate')
            ->will($this->returnValue(false));

    $this->specify('contact should not send', function () use
(&$model) {
            expect($model->contact(null), false);
            expect($model->contact('admin@example.com'), false);
    });

}
```

Now, let's run our tests again, and we will see the screenshot shown here:

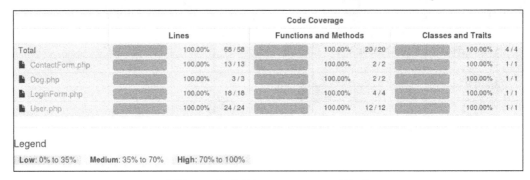

	Code Coverage								
	Lines			Functions and Methods			Classes and Traits		
Total		100.00%	58 / 58		100.00%	20 / 20		100.00%	4 / 4
ContactForm.php		100.00%	13 / 13		100.00%	2 / 2		100.00%	1 / 1
Dog.php		100.00%	3 / 3		100.00%	2 / 2		100.00%	1 / 1
LoginForm.php		100.00%	18 / 18		100.00%	4 / 4		100.00%	1 / 1
User.php		100.00%	24 / 24		100.00%	12 / 12		100.00%	1 / 1

Legend

Low: 0% to 35%   **Medium:** 35% to 70%   **High:** 70% to 100%

We've reached 100 percent coverage! Yay!

I'll leave it to you to fix the remaining errors. Certain situations might be hard to cover, and you may need additional hints and suggestions on how to restructure your tests.

Aggregating functional tests to unit tests

Now that we've seen what is going on in our unit tests and how to visually understand if we have effectively covered as much as we could, we can move to the functional tests that we wrote previously.

As we saw earlier, we can just add the functional suite to the command line for generating the aggregated reports.

```
$ ../vendor/bin/codecept run unit,functional --coverage
```

We will also see that by omitting the suites we will end up with the same result, but we don't know when the Codeception developers will merge all the three suites into a single coverage report, so just keep this in mind and consult the documentation.

Our unit tests have covered the models in their entirety. Our functional tests should focus on the controllers. You should be able to spot that the login page and the REST module controller have not been covered completely. So, let's discuss these one by one.

The login page will display the missing coverage for the login and the logout action.

In the first case, it seems pretty easy to cover that. We have to make sure that we reach that action after logging in. So, let's add the following assertion right after the successful login at the end of the test file:

```
// tests/codeception/functional/LoginCept.php

$I->amGoingTo('ensure I cannot load the login page if I am logged
in');
$I->amOnPage('/index-test.php/login');
$I->seeCurrentUrlEquals('/index-test.php');
```

As we can see, we're using a few specific paths for testing the website. This isn't a problem when interacting with the Codeception REST module, but here we have to be verbose.

The other portion that we have to cover is a little more complex. Once we are logged in, notice that the logout button has a JS click event attached to it, and that will send a POST request to `/logout`.

Since PHPBrowser won't be able to read JS, nor will it have the ability to do a specific POST call, we won't be able to cover this piece of code. Don't even think about using `sendPost()` as it's a specific method, which comes from the REST module of Codeception.

The only solution for this is to leave the coverage of this bit to the acceptance tests or to WebDriver.

Due to the fact that acceptance and functional tests have not been merged, we can exclude this method from the coverage report by using `@codeCoverageIgnore`. However, make sure that this isn't a case anymore and discuss it with your colleagues before excluding the method coverage from all the tests.

The last part that we need to cover is the controller of the REST interface. Here, we have a mixed situation. We have uncovered the functions that are mostly a part of our framework, such as the anonymous function that performs the authentication and `checkAccess()`, we have a small bit in `actionUpdate()`, which forbids anything but a PUT, and we have another control statement in `actionSearch()`, which controls who can search what.

In the first two cases we'll gladly avoid them from getting covered, as we've explicitly excluded the framework files which these two are part of.

For `actionUpdate()`, we'll find out that we won't even need a specific check, as Yii already defines the type of HTTP call that is allowed against the default REST interfaces.

We can add a test that ensures that we can't perform a POST on the interface and it can be added to any of the already present tests. This could be something along the lines of the following code block:

```
// tests/codeception/functional/UserAPIEndpointsCept.php

// I must be authenticated at this point.
$I->amGoingTo('I cannot update using POST');
$I->sendPOST('users/' . $userId);
$I->seeResponseCodeIs(405);
```

Lastly, we want to ensure that the user can only search for his own username to get the ID, as we outlined in *Chapter 6, Testing the API – PHPBrowser to the Rescue*. In order to do this, we can simply add something similar to the code block shown here:

```
// tests/codeception/functional/UserAPICept.php

// I must be authenticated at this point.
$I->amGoingTo('ensure I cannot search someone else');
$I->sendGET('users/search/someoneelse');
$I->seeResponseCodeIs(403);
```

If we run the tests with coverage, then we'll get a 100 percent on all the files that we wanted to see the coverage on.

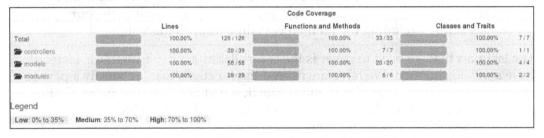

		Code Coverage					
		Lines		Functions and Methods		Classes and Traits	
Total		100.00%	126 / 126	100.00%	33 / 33	100.00%	7 / 7
controllers		100.00%	39 / 39	100.00%	7 / 7	100.00%	1 / 1
models		100.00%	58 / 58	100.00%	20 / 20	100.00%	4 / 4
modules		100.00%	28 / 29	100.00%	6 / 6	100.00%	2 / 2

Legend
Low: 0% to 35% **Medium:** 35% to 70% **High:** 70% to 100%

The final overview of the coverage for unit and functional tests

Generating acceptance tests' coverage report

Now that we've seen what to make of our coverage reports, we'll quickly look at the configuration that will help us in obtaining the coverage reports for the acceptance tests.

These coverage reports might not be the most important ones, but if constructed correctly, then they should prove that our scenarios are well written. Normally, the focus of acceptance tests is on ensuring browser cross- and preserving retro-compatibility.

As we've seen in *Chapter 7, Having Fun Doing Browser Testing*, Codeception talks to the Selenium standalone server, which in turn launches the browser and performs the required tests through the browser driver. Because of this architecture, the c3 project has been created, which basically listens to the browser calls and understands which bit of our code is being executed remotely.

So, first of all, let's get c3. We can either download it from Composer or from the official website (`https://github.com/Codeception/c3`) by running this command from the root of the project:

```
$ wget https://raw.github.com/Codeception/c3/2.0/c3.php
```

If you're downloading it through Composer, then you'll have to add some additional instructions to the `composer.json` file. You should take the official documentation as the main reference point.

Once you have it, include it in the `index-test.php` file:

```
// web/index-test.php
//...
include_once __DIR__ . '/c3.php';
$config = require(__DIR__ . '/../tests/codeception/config/acceptance.
php');
(new yii\web\Application($config))->run();
```

With this, we have hooked c3 to Yii. Now, we just need to make Codeception aware of it. So open the `codeception.yml` file, and add the following options to the `coverage` section of the file:

```
# tests/codeception.yml
# ...
coverage:
    enabled: true
    remote: true
    remote_config: ../tests/codeception.yml
    # whitelist:
    # blacklist:
    c3_url: 'https://basic-dev.yii2.sandbox/index-test.php/'
```

We need to enable the remote coverage, set the configuration of the file by using `remote_config`, and then specify the URL c3 should be listening on.

The detailed explanation of the remote code coverage and its configuration can be read from the official documentation of Codeception, which can be found at http://codeception.com/docs/11-Codecoverage, and from the README.md file, which is either located in the tests/ directory of your project or at https://github.com/yiisoft/yii2-app-basic/tree/master/tests#remote-code-coverage.

Now, all our remote calls will go through the index-test.php file, and they will use c3 to generate the coverage data.

Additionally, we may want to get a trimmed down report for specific acceptance tests, and in our case, we can decide to focus our attention only on the controllers that are being hit, and then choose to remove any reporting for the models.

In order to do so, consider what we already have in the main configuration file. We just need to add the following to our acceptance.suite.yml file:

```
# tests/codeception/acceptance.suite.yml
coverage:
    blacklist:
        include:
            - ../models/*
```

At this point, you can generate the reports separately by using the code block shown here:

```
$ ../vendor/bin/codecept run acceptance --coverage-html
```

You can also do this by simply running the tests for the whole suite, as follows:

```
$ ../vendor/bin/codecept run --coverage-html
```

As we saw earlier, both of these methods will generate a separate report for the acceptance tests. It might happen that in the future this is no longer valid, so be sure to head over to the official documentation and check that.

Once we generate the reports, we will notice two things: the tests with the coverage report might take ages, so we don't want to run this every time we make a change to the interface. Secondly, we will have to cover the missing logout test that we have highlighted before.

So, let's go to our LoginCept.php file and add what's missing.

```
$I->amGoingTo('ensure I cannot load the login page if I am logged in');
$I->amOnPage('/index-test.php/login');
```

```
$I->seeCurrentUrlEquals('/index-test.php');

$I->amGoingTo('try to logout');
$I->click('Logout (admin)');
if (method_exists($I, 'wait')) {
    $I->wait(3); // only for selenium
}
$I->seeCurrentUrlEquals('/index-test.php');
```

Please note that we need to be very specific while using the URLs, just as we were with the functional tests.

Once this is done, we should find ourselves with the complete coverage of all the suites.

In the next section, we'll see what else we can generate, and then we'll take it to the next level with the aid of automation in the next chapter.

Improving our code with the aid of additional tools

In addition to code coverage and test reports, we have a range of additional tools, which we can use for improving the quality of our code.

The two tools that we're going to talk about are the check style and the cyclomatic complexity through the C.R.A.P. index.

We are going to add more examples and tools to these in *Chapter 9, Eliminating Stress with the Help of Automation*, as each command would require too much knowledge from the developer's side, and it is something that can be automated and triggered by the flick of a switch.

PHP Checkstyle (PHPCS)is a great tool, albeit it is rather complex at first . This will help us in maintaining a style of code that is uniform for all developers. You might care too much about this, and I've seen situations where decisions on which style to use have resulted in a big fight. However, the benefits of this are quite evident, as it forces the developers to control their style of coding. When used with the cyclomatic complexity, it can standardize the code and avoid any situation involving intricate and difficult code.

There are some already existing code standards available for your use and these have been configured according to your needs. PHPCS only needs a reference for the configuration file or the name of the standard to follow.

We are going to install and use Yii 2 own code standards, which you can use as a base for specifying the rules that are more suited to your needs.

You can install the Yii 2 code standards by using Composer, which will include the actual binary that we need as a dependency:

```
// composer.json
    "require-dev": {
        . . .
            "yiisoft/yii2-coding-standards": "*"
```

Once we have installed both of them, we can invoke them through the console by using the following command:

```
$ vendor/bin/phpcs \--standard=vendor/yiisoft/yii2-coding-standards/Yii2/
ruleset.xml \ --extensions=php \--ignore=autoload.php \models controllers
modules
```

The last three arguments are the folders that we want PHPCS to scan.

If you want to improve your code, then you should make use of the C.R.A.P. index, which is included in the coverage reports generated by Codeception. In the following chapter, we'll see how the cyclomatic complexity index can be used for basing the decisions for modifying your code.

The C.R.A.P. index has been designed for analyzing and predicting the amount of effort, pain, and time required for maintaining an existing body of code.

It is mathematically defined as shown here:

$C.R.A.P.(m) = comp(m)\hat{}2 * (1 - cov(m)/100)\hat{}3 + comp(m)$

Where *comp(m)* is the cyclomatic complexity, and *cov(m)* is the test code coverage provided by the automated tests. The cyclomatic complexity is calculated as 1 plus the number of unique decisions in the method.

A low C.R.A.P. index indicates a relatively low change and maintenance risk, because it's either not too complex or sufficiently covered by tests. To keep it practical, if your method is a straight sequence of calls, then it is likely that it will have a C.R.A.P. index that is close to 1. The more `if`, `for`, and `while` clauses it has, the more complex it will be, and hence it will have a higher C.R.A.P. index.

This is where testing lets the potential problems emerge and points you in the direction that you should be taking for keeping your code maintainable and modular.

Summary

In this chapter, we've discussed the basic steps needed for configuring and generating the code coverage for the project. We've seen how to use the reports generated for discovering potential problems with the code. We've also covered some additional tools for improving our code quality.

In *Chapter 9, Eliminating Stress with the Help of Automation*, we'll complete this journey. We will discuss the topic of additional tools, how to integrate them into a continuous integration system, and then display the results for better access and browsing.

Eliminating Stress with the Help of Automation

So far, we've covered almost every aspect of what testing in practice is. We've learned what can be done with Codeception at all the levels of testing: unit, functional, and acceptance. We've covered additional resources on how to improve and debug your tests while looking at architectural choices and long-term considerations.

To keep it short, in this chapter, we're going to take the final step, which is nowadays considered as the best practice: continuous integration.

We are going to understand what a continuous integration system is, and what the choices that we have are. We'll also start working with Jenkins.

In this chapter, we will discuss everything that we need to install and configure. We will run our builds and obtain the required level of automation for our project. We'll cover the following topics:

- Automating the build process
- Creating the required build files
- Configuring the Jenkins build
- Going forward

Automating the build process

There are two aspects that you should always take into consideration when planning and implementing your tests. Firstly, 100 percent code coverage won't help you in removing the possibility of having or introducing a bug, which means that exploratory manual testing will always be needed, and it will have to be factored in while writing your initial draft of the master test plan. Secondly, until now, all the tests and reports that we've generated for such a small project can be run manually by whoever changes the code.

When the size of your code starts to grow and you start to support hundreds of classes and multi-faceted frontend functionalities, when your code lives past the first month and more than one developer will need to access it over and over again, all the knowledge related to tests and how they work or what kind of information can be extracted from them will become more and more difficult to maintain. The worst part is that most likely nobody will use it without any struggle.

Here, you have two choices: accept the fate that your tests will be long forgotten and nobody will know what's been covered and what needs to be covered, or start automating all this by forcing some sort of automated code revision, which might trigger reports and e-mails to warn about anything that can potentially go wrong, or has already gone wrong.

Introducing continuous integration systems

Extreme Programming (XP) has introduced the concept of **continuous integration (CI)**. Nowadays, it's used in many companies as a part of their QA procedures, regardless of the practice adopted.

Whether frequent integration is better than continuous integration is something I'd prefer to leave out of this discussion. The main difference between the two is based on the frequency at which the integration happens. On top of this, CI has been conceived to be a part of TDD, and it is specifically aimed at running tests before merging any features into the active branch. This is done to ensure that the new functionality won't break the existing one.

Systems like Jenkins (formerly known as Hudson), Bamboo, CruiseControl, and Travis, have been created so that the work of the different developers can be *integrated* and tested before being shipped. This also ensures that certain quality standards are reached so that we can avoid introducing incoherence in the code base, and we can report the results to the developers.

These software systems perform a multitude of tasks. They're made in such a way that they can support any programming language and testing framework.

Usually, they're built for providing a flexible way of defining your integration work flow: code check out, preparation, build (which usually includes testing and other quality assurance-related tasks), report publishing, artifact creation, and eventually deployment. All of these steps can be controlled within the system and/or through scripting of various types. For instance, you can use Ant or Maven in Travis, Bamboo, or Jenkins. Apart from the basic functionality, several plugins are normally available in these systems for extending the functionality of integrating additional third-party applications, libraries, and services.

Before getting into the nitty-gritty details of configuring the continuous integration system of our choice, we may want to first see what's available and how we can choose.

Available systems

There are a number of CI systems, and many of them have been created specifically for certain programming languages; therefore, they can perform only a restricted set of operations.

The more complex the system is, the more time it takes to prepare it to behave as we want it to, but you'll have the ability to perform as many functions as required, and you will also have the ability to switch them on or off on a per-project basis.

The most well-known system is Jenkins. It is an open source system (`http://jenkins-ci.org`). It was forked in 2011 from Hudson, after a dispute with Oracle. It is a CI system written in Java, and it became popular as an alternative to CruiseControl. It has always been regarded as the most polyfunctional CI system available. This is also because its huge community provides hundreds of different plugins for any kind of functionality.

The only problem I see with Jenkins, apart from configuring it, is hosting it, although, installing and maintaining it has always been easy for me.

You might be unable to host the system yourself, so you may want to look for something that provides a hosted solution. Bamboo is another choice that is said to be particularly straightforward if you are migrating from Jenkins. It also provides out-of-the-box integration with other Atlassian products, such as Jira, BitBucket, HipChat, and so on.

As a matter of choice, we'll be looking into Jenkins, installing the required plugins, and then creating the build by using the Apache Ant scripts.

Installing and configuring Jenkins

There isn't much to be said about the installation of Jenkins. As the installation page shows, it's cross-compatible and it can be run on operating systems, such as Windows, Linux, Unix, and Docker. For more information, check out `https://wiki.jenkins-ci.org/display/JENKINS/Installing+Jenkins`.

 It's important to remember that its only requirement is Java, so you should have up-to-date versions of JDK and JRE.

Most distributions already package Jenkins and provide it with their official package repositories, thereby solving most of the problems of dependencies.

The installation on *nix systems will create its own dedicated user `Jenkins`, which will be used for doing all the operations that will be run through its interface. Never run Jenkins as a superuser. This can cause security issues. The workspace where the projects will be checked out is normally located at `/var/lib/jenkins/home/workspace`, which you can inspect manually if something goes wrong.

When started, Jenkins will be listening on port `8080` (not always, be sure to read the post-installation instructions, if any, or check the opened ports using `netstat -ltn` on Linux), and it will be accessible from the web browser.

 If you want to expose your service to a wider audience, then you might want to install a proxy in order to serve it from port `80`, with whichever hostname you want. We won't cover this aspect, but Jenkins provides additional documentation on how to achieve this.

So, let's open `http://<yourhostname>:8080` in our browser, and let's start configuring the basics.

Understanding the Jenkins organization

Before doing this, you may need to understand how Jenkins is organized. If you are already experienced with it, then you may want to skip over to the next section.

There are only two sections that you need to keep an eye out for:

- The jobs list
- The management panel

The first one is where you will normally land, and it is what you will be working on most of the time.

In the Jenkins terminology, a **job** is a specific set of rules and operations that needs to be performed in a specific project. You can have different jobs for the same project, which perform slightly or completely different operations, and these can be triggered sequentially.

A **build** is the process of executing a job. We will cover this and see what we can achieve with a single build by configuring the various aspects of the job. The build can result in the creation of one or more artefacts, deploy the build result somewhere or trigger some other job or process within Jenkins itself, or outside of it.

You need to fix Jenkins' security immediately after installing it, unless you will be the only person accessing it and the server where it's installed will have no external access, it's probably better to navigate to `http://jenkins:8080/ configureSecurity/`.

You can set up whichever authentication system you want, using PAM, LDAP, or its internal user database. We will be using the latter, but remember that if you're willing to do something a bit stronger or interconnected, there may be additional steps that you may need to follow. Most of the interface forms have a few small info buttons that you can use to display some information, as shown in the following screenshot:

View of the **Configure Global Security** page with an open info box

The second aspect that requires a little thinking from your side is how Jenkins will be accessing and checking your repository.

Any major online repository provider, such as GitHub and BitBucket will let you create a so-called **deployment key**, which is used for a read-only access to the repository.

For anything more complex, such as merging and pushing your branches, you would need to set up its own user, as shown in the following screenshot:

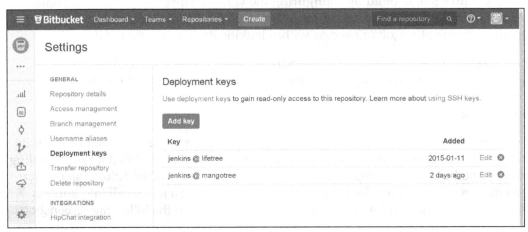

The deployment keys setup page in BitBucket, available from the settings of each repository

If you have more repositories that are hosted by different places, then you need to set up as many credentials as needed for Jenkins. This can be accomplished by going to http://jenkins:8080/credential-store/ (or **Home | Credentials | Global Credentials**). As you can see, there's a lot behind the scenes, so feel free to explore and read the documentation for understanding what's needed. Normally starting with the setup of the global credentials may be enough, but there are cases where a non-global configuration is needed.

In order to do so, we need to create the SSH key pairs for the user jenkins first.

```
peach ~ $ sudo -s
root peach # su jenkins -
jenkins peach $ cd ~
jenkins ~ $ pwd
/var/lib/jenkins
jenkins ~ $ ssh-keygen
Generating public/private rsa key pair.
Enter file in which to save the key (/var/lib/jenkins/.ssh/id_rsa):
Enter passphrase (empty for no passphrase):
Enter same passphrase again:
```

```
Your identification has been saved in /var/lib/jenkins/.ssh/id_rsa.
Your public key has been saved in /var/lib/jenkins/.ssh/id_rsa.pub.
The key fingerprint is:
ff:be:b1:ee:c2:69:82:96:00:e4:9d:dd:67:cf:1e:d7 jenkins@mangotree
The key's randomart image is:
+---[RSA 2048]----+
|                 |
|                 |
| . . o. .        |
|+ . *.oo  .      |
|.o o .o+S. E     |
|+ o    .+o       |
|+*. . o.         |
|+. . .           |
|                 |
+-----------------+
```

Now that you have your SSH key, you need to grab the public key, which is stored at /var/lib/jenkins/.ssh/id_rsa.pub, and then copy it to your repository as a deployment key. You can copy it to the clipboard by using the following command:

```
root jenkins # xclip -sel clip < /var/lib/jenkins/.ssh/id_rsa.pub
```

This has been done through the root user because the jenkins user won't have the X display setup in its environment and this is likely to cause the error shown here:

```
No protocol specified
Error: Can't open display: :0
```

 If you are on a headless server, then you won't have many choices. You can either scp on the file to your local machine or cat the file and then paste it in the browser manually.

Now that you have your deployment key set up, you need to go back to Jenkins and then navigate to the credentials store. Once there, set the username as jenkins (which is the system's user name), and set the private key as From the Jenkins master ~/.ssh.

The following sections will cover the installation of additional plugins and the configuration of the job.

Installing the required plugins

Now that you have covered the basic configuration of Jenkins, you need to install the required plugins so that everything works as expected.

This section is normally handled easily by Jenkins. There's a project that is specifically for the PHP projects on Jenkins. You can find it at `http://jenkins-php.org`. Not only does the project list the following plugins, but it also lists a meta plugin, which is available on Jenkins, and it will download all the required plug-ins.

- **Checkstyle**: This is used for processing the PHP_CodeSniffer log files in the Checkstyle format
- **Clover PHP**: This is used for processing the PHPUnit's Clover XML log file
- **Crap4J**: This is used for processing the PHPUnit's Crap4J XML log file
- **DRY**: This is used for processing the phpcpd log files in the PMD-CPD format
- **HTML Publisher**: This is used for publishing the documentation generated by phpDox
- **JDepend**: This is used for processing the PHP_Depend log files in the JDepend format
- **Plot**: This is used for processing the phploc CSV output
- **PMD**: This is used for processing the PHPMD log files in the PMD format
- **Violations**: This is used for processing the various log files
- **xUnit**: This is used for processing the PHPUnit's JUnit XML log file

The preceding list is taken from `http://jenkins-php.org/installation.html`, and it might change in the future, so keep that in mind.

If you navigate to **Manage Jenkins | Manage Plugins**, then you can search for the plugin `php` and select **Install without restart**. When you are on the installation page, select the **Restart Jenkins when installation is complete and no jobs are running** option (sometimes the installation page does not refresh itself automatically, so you might have to refresh the page; a list of plugins will get installed even if you navigate away from this page).

Now, you need to install the tools needed by these plugins, so open the `composer.json` file and then add the following to your `require-dev` section:

```
// composer.json
"phploc/phploc": "@stable",
```

```
"pdepend/pdepend": "@stable",
"phpmd/phpmd": "@stable",
"sebastian/phpcpd": "@dev",
"yiisoft/yii2-coding-standards": "*",
"theseer/phpdox": "@stable"
```

Now, run the `composer update` to install these effectively.

Creating the required build files

A part of the configuration of the build will be stored in Jenkins, but it's mostly for publishing the reports and the documentation (if you need it). We saw the actual configuration on how to run the various scripts in *Chapter 8, Analyzing Testing Information*. This is in the `build.xml` file. This default name can be picked up by Jenkins automatically. This can be configured, but it's pointless to do so unless you already have a file with that name.

The build file should sit at the root of the project repository, and it should have a valid XML.

The language we are going to use to write the build file is Apache Ant. There are either more complex solutions, such as Maven, or more ad-hoc solutions such as Phing for this, but I still prefer Ant. This is because it's simple and flexible (it's verbose, but once you've written it, there isn't much to be said). It also allows you to run anything that is not specific for a particular language.

We're going to create the build file by copying the basic structure from the `jenkins-php` project (available at `http://jenkins-php.org/automation.html`), and then by amending it with the corrections that I'll explain in the next few paragraphs. I'll be splitting the functionality of Composer, Yii, and Codeception in separate files, while the main functionality (from `jenkins-php`) will remain as it is.

Understanding the basic Ant structure

Ant is quite simple because it's a collection of directives. The root of the XML is a `<project>` tag, which contains a series of `<target>` tags that can be called from the Jenkins job, and you can choose the `<property>` option for defining the properties, and then choose the `<include>` statements for including separate files.

There is no default name for the targets, but the main target is usually called `build`. It comes with a series of dependencies, which trigger the other targets sequentially.

Each directive has a series of additional attributes and tags, and these can be nested in them. The user contributed directives can also be downloaded separately for these (and most of the Linux distributions provide the common ones in a separate package). This can help you in avoiding the effort that is put in when you have to create these by hand. For instance, you can use this for archiving and packaging a collection of files, which are normally wrappers for the actual command-line tools.

Remember that Ant is not an imperative programming language, so check its documentation if you want to extend and modify the language.

The documentation for the core Ant directives is available online at `http://ant.apache.org/manual/`, and it's probably a good starting point for understanding it.

Adjusting the build.xml file

Compared to the file you have copied from `jenkins-php`, we are going to keep most of the targets, albeit the `phpunit` target, which can be safely deleted. This is because we're going to switch to a custom target specifically for Codeception. The rest of the changes will be made in separate files, and they will be discussed after this.

The most important changes that need to be made are relative to the folders you want these programs to work on. Every single command accepts different arguments, so include all the directories you want. Let's start amending the first target, which will do a syntax check of all the files that we specify:

```
<target name="lint" description="Perform syntax check of
  sourcecode files">
    <apply executable="php" failonerror="true">
        <arg value="-l" />

        <fileset dir="${basedir}/models">
            <include name="**/*.php" />
            <modified />
        </fileset>
        <fileset dir="${basedir}/modules">
            <include name="**/*.php" />
            <modified />
        </fileset>
        <fileset dir="${basedir}/controllers">
            <include name="**/*.php" />
            <modified />
        </fileset>
        <fileset dir="${basedir}/tests">
```

```
            <include name="**/*.php" />
            <modified />
         </fileset>
      </apply>
</target>
```

Next, we can add our code directories to be picked up by phploc, which will give us an idea of the complexity of our project:

```
<target name="phploc-ci"
         depends="prepare"
         description="Measure project size using PHPLOC and log
            result in CSV and XML format. Intended for usage within
            a continuous integration environment.">
      <exec executable="${toolsdir}phploc">
         <arg value="--count-tests" />
         <arg value="--log-csv" />
         <arg path="${basedir}/build/logs/phploc.csv" />
         <arg value="--log-xml" />
         <arg path="${basedir}/build/logs/phploc.xml" />
         <arg path="${basedir}/models" />
         <arg path="${basedir}/controllers" />
         <arg path="${basedir}/modules" />
         <arg path="${basedir}/tests" />
      </exec>
</target>
```

pdepend uses a different syntax in defining new directories; as you can see, if you need to make changes, you will need to invoke the commands' help manually:

```
<target name="pdepend"
         depends="prepare"
         description="Calculate software metrics using PHP_Depend
            and log result in XML format. Intended for usage within
            a continuous integration environment.">
      <exec executable="${toolsdir}pdepend">
         <arg value="--jdepend-xml=${basedir}/build/
            logs/jdepend.xml" />
         <arg value="--jdepend-chart=${basedir}/build/
            pdepend/dependencies.svg" />
         <arg value="--overview-pyramid=${basedir}/build/
            pdepend/overview-pyramid.svg" />
         <arg path="${basedir}/models,${basedir}/controllers,
            ${basedir}/modules,${basedir}/tests" />
      </exec>
</target>
```

Next in line is PHP Mess Detection (PHPMD), which will help us keep the code clean and tidy. Once again, the syntax is slightly different than the previous ones:

```xml
<target name="phpmd-ci"
        depends="prepare"
        description="Perform project mess detection using PHPMD
            and log result in XML format. Intended for usage within
            a continuous integration environment.">
    <exec executable="${toolsdir}phpmd">
        <arg path="${basedir}/models,${basedir}/
            controllers,${basedir}/modules" />
        <arg value="xml" />
        <arg path="${basedir}/build/phpmd.xml" />
        <arg value="--reportfile" />
        <arg path="${basedir}/build/logs/pmd.xml" />
    </exec>
</target>
```

PHP Code Sniffer (PHPCS) can be also taken as an additional and more important step for linting your code. As explained, we also need to specify the specific Yii coding standard:

```xml
<target name="phpcs-ci"
        depends="prepare"
        description="Find coding standard violations using
            PHP_CodeSniffer and log result in XML format. Intended
            for usage within a continuous integration environment.">
    <exec executable="${toolsdir}phpcs" output="/dev/null">
        <arg value="--report=checkstyle" />
        <arg value="--report-file=${basedir}/build/
            logs/checkstyle.xml" />
        <arg value="--standard=${basedir}/vendor/yiisoft/yii2-
            coding-standards/Yii2/ruleset.xml" />
        <arg value="--extensions=php" />
        <arg value="--ignore=autoload.php" />
        <arg path="${basedir}/models" />
        <arg path="${basedir}/controllers" />
        <arg path="${basedir}/modules" />
        <arg path="${basedir}/tests" />
    </exec>
</target>
```

The last one is PHP Copy-Paste Detector (PHPCPD), which does exactly what it says on the label:

```
<target name="phpcpd-ci"
        depends="prepare"
        description="Find duplicate code using PHPCPD and log
            result in XML format. Intended for usage within a
            continuous integration environment.">
    <exec executable="${toolsdir}phpcpd">
        <arg value="--log-pmd" />
        <arg path="${basedir}/build/logs/pmd-cpd.xml" />
        <arg path="${basedir}/models" />
        <arg path="${basedir}/controllers" />
        <arg path="${basedir}/modules" />
    </exec>
</target>
```

As you have probably noticed, some of the targets that I've pasted here are the `-ci` targets. These targets are required by Jenkins in order to generate all the necessary reports. We will pick these up and publish them in our build later. Remember to mirror the changes on the other targets as well; I have excluded them here to avoid redundancy.

In addition to these changes, it's worth noticing that I've selected the Yii 2 CheckStyle rule set for validating the syntax. This step is quite useful for maintaining the overall code style and for keeping it in sync with the one used by the developers of the framework, and cross-team.

Now that we've made the basic changes, let's go to the Composer, Yii, and the Codeception files.

Preparing the environment for the build

The `build` command, which is the default invoked target, has a chain of dependencies that will sequentially trigger the `prepare` target, run some other targets for the build, run the tests, and then generate the required documentation with phpDox.

The `prepare` target depends on the `clean` target. These two steps will clean up the environment, generate the required folder structure to accommodate the results that will be produced by the following steps, and set some properties to avoid invoking the target twice.

For instance, the `prepare` target has the following property set at the end:

```
<property name="prepare.done" value="true"/>
```

While the target definition is:

```
<target name="prepare"
        unless="prepare.done"
        depends="clean, composer.composer, yii.migrate-all"
        description="Prepare for build">
```

It has now become clear that *unless* the property is set, we can execute the content of the target. The same thing happens with the `clean` target.

In these two targets, we need to update the list of directories that are cleaned and recreated every time the job is run. You should, at least, have the following directories, and you can also include any other directories that are relevant to your project for `clean`.

```
<target name="clean"
        unless="clean.done"
        description="Cleanup build artifacts">
    <delete dir="${basedir}/runtime/*"/>
    <delete dir="${basedir}/web/assets/*"/>
    <delete dir="${basedir}/vendor"/>
    <delete dir="${basedir}/build/api"/>
    <delete dir="${basedir}/build/logs"/>
    <delete dir="${basedir}/build/pdepend"/>
    <delete dir="${basedir}/build/phpdox"/>
    <delete dir="${basedir}/tests/codeception/_output"/>
        <property name="clean.done" value="true"/>
</target>
```

And for `prepare`, the following directories will be recreated:

```
<target name="prepare"
        unless="prepare.done"
        depends="clean, composer.composer, yii.migrate-all"
        description="Prepare for build">
    <mkdir dir="${basedir}/build/api"/>
    <mkdir dir="${basedir}/build/logs"/>
    <mkdir dir="${basedir}/build/pdepend"/>
    <mkdir dir="${basedir}/build/phpdox"/>
    <mkdir dir="${basedir}/tests/codeception/_output"/>
        <property name="prepare.done" value="true"/>
</target>
```

Adding the required configuration settings

Before we start adding our custom files, we need to add some of the configuration files, which some of the executables, namely phpmd and PHPDox, will expect to be in the /build directory.

The jenkins-php project will provide most of these configuration files, and these can be copied from http://jenkins-php.org/configuration.html.

In case of phpmd, you can adjust the level of the cyclomatic complexity threshold.

```xml
<!-- build/phpmd.xml -->
<rule ref="rulesets/codesize.xml/CyclomaticComplexity">
    <priority>1</priority>
    <properties>
        <property name="reportLevel" value="7" />
    </properties>
</rule>
```

The default value is normally 10, but the suggested value is 5.

For PHPDox, the story is a little complex. The current configuration is not particularly flexible, so I've decided to go through the longest possible route, which is, generating the skeleton file with the help of the following command:

$ vendor/bin/phpdox --skel > build/phpdox.xml

This created a file that has all the documented options, and from there, I created my own configuration file:

```xml
<?xml version="1.0" encoding="utf-8" ?>
<!-- build/phpdox.xml -->
<phpdox xmlns="http://xml.phpdox.net/config" silent="false">
    <project name="Yii2" source="${basedir}/.." workdir=
      "${basedir}/phpdox">

        <collector publiconly="false">
            <include mask="${phpDox.project.source}/models/*.php"
              />
            <include mask="${phpDox.project.source}/modules/*.php"
              />
            <include mask="${phpDox.project.source}/
              controllers/*.php" />
            <include mask="${phpDox.project.source}/vendor/
              yiisoft/yii2/*.php" />
```

```
        </collector>

        <generator output="${basedir}/api">
            <build engine="html" enabled="true">
                <file extension="html" />
            </build>
        </generator>

    </project>
</phpdox>
```

Regardless of my efforts, the current version that I'm using (0.7) had a bug that caused it to crash when run from Jenkins. This has been fixed in the current dev-master version, but this has caused other problems for me. I'm pretty sure that you should be fine when the next version will be released. In our case, the documentation is less critical from the perspective of the non-working tests.

Adding Composer, Yii, and Codeception support in Ant

Now we need to integrate the changes that are needed to prepare our application for testing. We will be using Composer to install the required dependencies and Yii to run the needed migrations. After this we will need support for Codeception, as it's the main tool for running the tests.

As we've seen in the definition of `prepare`, the target is dependent on `clean`, `composer.composer` and `yii.migrate-all`.

The first target is taken from `https://github.com/shrikeh/ant-phptools`, which provides a wrapper for Composer. It's not the best, but it was the only one that showed up on a quick search. The package does what it does quite well, and it's dependent on a properties file called `composer.properties`, and an example of it is provided by the project author.

> There are some built-in properties that are accessible in an Ant script, which can be useful for understanding, for instance, the current directory and building up the appropriate paths in a more distributable fashion. This is available at `http://ant.apache.org/manual/properties.html`.

Calling the `composer.composer` target will install Composer, if not found in the specified directory, and use it to update all the dependencies. I would prefer if it wiped the installation directory of the dependencies and then ran `composer install`. Unfortunately, that's the only way to install the dependencies defined in the `composer.lock`, instead of updating them.

 If you have any doubts about the differences between `composer.lock` and `composer.json`, feel free to step back for a second, and skim through *Chapter 2, Tooling up for Testing*.

I've put the `composer.xml` and the `composer.properties` file in the `/build` directory, and I've added the following at the beginning of the project defined in `build.xml`.

```
<include file="${basedir}/build/composer.xml" as="composer"/>
```

Now, we can add the dependency of `composer.composer` to the list of the targets defined in the `prepare` target without any problems.

The second step is resetting the database to a state that we can use, and we will do it by re-running all of the migrations and applying all of the missing ones.

For this, I've created a simple Ant project. You can place it in your `/build` directory, which you can download from `https://github.com/ThePeach/Yii2-Ant`. The project provides a wrapper for the Yii CLI interface for running the migrations.

I won't go into the details of this project, as it's simple and it can be understood quite easily.

We can include it like we did in the Composer project earlier, as follows:

```
<!-- build.xml -->
<include file="${basedir}/build/yii.xml" as="yii"/>
```

You can invoke it either by calling the ready-made target `migrate-all`, as we did for the dependencies of `prepare` in our `build.xml`, or by calling the `migrate` MacroDef the way you want:

```
<migrate exec="${yii.script}" action="down"/>
<migrate exec="${yii.script}" action="up"/>
<migrate exec="${yii.tests.script}" action="down"/>
<migrate exec="${yii.tests.script}" action="up"/>
```

Ant has to extend its basic syntax, which defines new tasks like MacroDef. You can read more about this in the official Apache Ant documentation, which can be found at `https://ant.apache.org/manual/Tasks/macrodef.html`.

The `migrate` action will always pass `all` as an argument to the `yii` script, and this is enough for what we need to achieve, but this could be improved.

Codeception is added in a similar way. You can grab a copy from the repository I've created at `https://github.com/ThePeach/CodeCeption-Ant`.

This Ant project provides a main target called `run-tests`, which you can execute without worrying too much about the parameters and such. You can also dynamically pass some parameters at run time to fine-tune the invocation of Codeception, such as `codeception.suites` and `codeception.options`.

```
$ ant -Dcodeception.suites=unit -Dcodeception.options=--coverage-html
build
```

If not set, these will be assigned an empty value and `--xml --coverage-xml --coverage-html` respectively.

Configuring the Jenkins build

The easiest way to configure the build is by starting with the `jenkins-php` project template. You can always import it separately and integrate it with your own project later.

The *Integration* page available at the `jenkins-php` website (`http://jenkins-php.org/integration.html`) will explain how to import the project. Remember to adjust the parameters to your own configuration.

Now go to the dashboard, click on the new project **jenkins-php**, and then select **Configure** from the menu.

If you've never used Jenkins, then you might get a little scared by the length of the configuration page. However, there are only three sections that you need to keep in mind, and we'll cover them now.

Generic build settings

Generic build settings contains settings for the enable/disable switch for the build, how many builds to keep, when to discard the build and the repository configuration, and so on.

If you're using Git, then you will have the ability to configure almost anything, such as being able to merge branches, committing and pushing back integrated changes, and so on.

We will just need to specify the branch as `*/master` and the deployment key as we what saved before, from our repository provider.

Build settings

The build settings are the only thing that you need to care about when deciding what to run; here you specify the target names and any additional options.

In our case, this is `build`, and by clicking **Advanced**, we can fill in the **Properties** field with `codeception.suites=unit`. This will allow us to run a test build without having to wait for long.

Postbuild settings

This is the longest section of the configuration. All the steps that will be performed for publishing the reports in the dashboard of the build, such as linking the documentation that you need to the various pieces, choosing what the thresholds required to decide are, and deciding when to mark the job failed, and so on are defined here.

The default threshold values defined here are quite high, so there isn't much that you should be worried about.

The only changes that we will need to make are regarding the reports generated by Codeception, which will provide the JUnit XML reports, the Clover XML reports, and the coverage in the HTML format.

Toward the end of the configuration page, you will find a section titled **Publish Clover PHP Coverage Report**, here update the Clover XML report path to `tests/codeception/_output/coverage.xml`, and the **Publish HTML Report** to `tests/codeception/_output/coverage/`. If you click on **Advanced panel**, then you will be able to modify the thresholds, and you can use them to decide how much coverage you require from your tests.

Just after this step, you will see **Publish xUnit test results report**, here change `PHPUnit-3.x Pattern` to `tests/codeception/_output/report.xml`. As you have done before, in the next step, you can configure the thresholds for the failed tests. By default, there shouldn't be any failed tests. So, all the fields will be set to 0. Do not change this setting, unless you want to live in shame.

Executing the job

Let's test everything and check if it is working as expected. Save the configuration, and click on **Build Now** to execute the job.

Once finished, you can head back to the page of the build, and then you will see the following graphs:

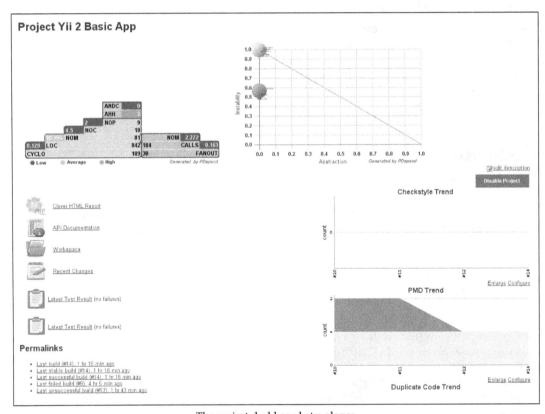

The project dashboard at a glance

Most of the graphs that appear on the right-hand side of the column are a quick way of understanding what triggered a failed build.

The two graphs, which are generated by PDepend, displayed at the very top show the so-called **Overview Pyramid** and the **Abstraction Instability Chart**. Both of them show interesting stats about your project, which you can depend on for taking some decisions in terms of performance, scalability, and maintainability.

> PDepend documentation provides further information about both of these graphs, and I highly recommend reading the following sources:
> - The Overview Pyramid at `http://pdepend.org/documentation/handbook/reports/overview-pyramid.html`
> - The Abstraction Instability Chart at `http://pdepend.org/documentation/handbook/reports/abstraction-instability-chart.html`

At this point, you should have all the tools required for stepping forward and implementing, improving and excelling at testing and at automating your projects.

Going forward

If you've managed to get to this point, then you might need to make some additional considerations.

As we've seen, automation incorporates a lot of reporting tools, suites for testing, and other projects to help you understand, improve, and analyze your project.

One of the biggest gripes of automation is the speed at which it performs all the tests.

There are techniques to halve the time it takes to perform these tests. While Jenkins and `jenkins-php` provide targets for running the targets in parallel, by executing `build-parallel`. With Codeception, the story is a bit different and you would need to take a different route by extending the Ant project we've created before. Codeception uses robo-paracept to parallelize the tests.

If you want to discover more about Codeception, then there's a nice article available at `http://codeception.com/docs/12-ParallelExecution`. You'll notice that it will work by marking groups of tests together and aggregating them so that Paracept will be able to run in parallel.

Summary

You've seen most of what you need to know about automation. The topic is quite vast, and we've covered Jenkins, how it works, and how it is configured. We've learned to make use of Ant to decide what to do, and how to drive your build. We've also looked at what is being generated by the build and displayed it in the Jenkins dashboard.

Index

Symbols

--coverage option 158
--report option 158

A

Abstraction Instability Chart
  URL 193
AcceptanceTester
  about 49
  implementing 49-51
  online documentation 51
acceptance tests
  about 35, 39
  creating 141, 142
  finalizing 150-152
  JavaScript interaction, adding 144-147
  modal window, implementing 142, 143
  multiple browsers, testing 152, 153
  Selenium limits 154
  server side, making work 144
  Yii 2 assets bundles, dealing with 148-150
actions, ActiveController 125
ActiveRecord class
  Gii code generation tool 83-87
  implementing 80
  migrations, dealing with 80-83
Ant directives
  URL 182
Attributes-Components-Capabilities (ACC)
  about 69
  URL 43
authenticators
  CompositeAuth 128
  HttpBasicAuth 128

HttpBearerAuth 128
QueryParamAuth 128

B

BDD specification testing
  using 103, 104
Behavior Driven Development (BDD) 1
black box testing 9
Bootstrap documentation
  URL 142
build 177
build files
  basic Ant structure 181
  build.xml file, adjusting 182-185
  Codeception support, adding in
    Ant 188-190
  Composer support, adding in Ant 188-190
  configuration settings, adding 187, 188
  creating 181
  environment, preparing 185
  Yii support, adding in Ant 188-190
build process, automating
  about 174
  CI systems 175
  continuous integration systems 174, 175
  Jenkins, configuring 176
  Jenkins, installing 176

C

calls
  listening, with observer 96, 97
Checkstyle plugin 180
CLI command line 29
Clover PHP plugin 180

code
  improving, with additional tools 169, 170
codecept build command 48
Codeception
  about 46
  basic concepts 47
  code generation arguments 62
  configuring 58-60
  features 54-56
  installing, in Yii 2 56, 57
  interacting with 61, 62
  migrations, on test database 62
  modular framework 47
  tests, creating 62
  types of tests 48
  URL 45
  working tests 60, 61
code coverage criteria
  branch coverage 156
  Change Risk Anti-Patterns (C.R.A.P.)
      Index 156
  class and trait coverage 156
  function and method coverage 156
  line coverage 156
  opcode coverage 156
  path coverage 156
components
  isolating, with stubs 93-96
component testing, of model
  data providers, using 75-77
  fixtures, using for preparing database 77-79
  methods inherited by IdentityInterface,
      testing 73-75
  performing 70, 71
  remaining tests, adding 80
  testing, for PHPUnit 72, 73
Composer
  about 20
  advanced web app 28
  basic web app 28
  CLI command line 29, 30
  composer.json file 22-24
  composer.lock file 22-24
  Exact version 25
  installing 20, 21
  packages 24-27
  Packagist 24-27

Range 25
URL 20
using 21
web app, creating 27-29
Wildcard 25
concepts, Codeception
  easy to debug 47
  easy to read 47
  easy to write 47
continuous integration (CI) 174
Crap4J plugin 180

D

data providers
  about 65
  using 75, 76
default web application
  documentation 33
  sample code 33
  structuring 32, 33
Defect Cost Increase (DCI) 6
deployment key 178
Design by Contract (DbC) specification
  about 10
  URL 10
development environment 18
Domain-driven Design (DDD) 10
double-checking 6
DRY plugin 180

E

enormous tests 40
external dependencies
  dealing with 91-93

F

FunctionalTester 51, 52
functional tests, in Yii 2
  about 107
  CEPTs 108
  CEPTs, improving 108-111
  fixtures, implementing 113-116
  pitfalls 116
  reusable page interactions, writing 112, 113

functional tests,, REST interfaces
  about 116-118
  API endpoints, defining 118
  implementing, for API 119, 120
fuzzy locator 139

G

Galen
  URL 154
Gii 83
Gii code generation tool 83-87
global fixtures
  used, for passing tests 88-90
Google Test Analytics software
  URL 11

H

headless 52
homebrew-php project
  URL 21
HTML Publisher plugin 180
HTTP Basic Auth 127

I

integration tests 35, 38

J

JDepend plugin 180
Jenkins
  configuring 176
  installing 176
  organization 176-179
  plugins, installing 180
  URL 175
Jenkins build
  build settings 191
  configuring 190
  generic build settings 191
  job, executing 192, 193
  postbuild settings 191
jenkins-php project
  URL 181
job 177

L

large tests 40
Late Static Binding 86
Linux Apache MariaDB PHP (LAMP) 19
local coverage report 158

M

MacroDef
  URL 190
maintainable unit tests
  BDD specification testing, using 103, 104
  writing 102
master test plan 42
medium tests 38
migrations
  about 63
  URL 63
mocking 97

O

OAuth
  URL 127
OAuth 2 127
Overview Pyramid
  URL 193

P

Packagist
  URL 25
PageObject 55
PHP Checkstyle (PHPCS) 169
PHP_Codesniffer
  URL 33
PHP-FIG
  URL 33
PHP manual
  URL 86
PHPUnit
  about 46
  URL, for documentation 95
Plot plugin 180
PMD plugin 180

project management
  approaches, testing 6-9
  involving 4, 5
  tasks, estimating 5, 6
  tests, generating 11
  tests, planning 11

Q

query parameter 127

R

RESTful web service, creating with Yii 2
  about 121
  access check and security layer,
    adding 126, 127
  authentication layer, building 128, 129
  controller, converting to REST
    controller 124-126
  existing actions, modifying 130
  modular code, writing in Yii 121
  module, creating with Gii 122-124
  modules, creating in Yii 2 124
  new endpoint, adding with
    parameters 131-133
roll back 82

S

scope 4
Selenium 135
Selenium WebDriver
  about 136
  installing 137
  running 137
  WebDriver-led tests, implementing 138-141
  Yii, configuring 137, 138
small tests 37
Specify 91, 103
StepObject 55
strict locator 139
stubbing 93

T

technical debt 4
test doubles 93

Test Driven Development (TDD) 1
testers, Codeception
  AcceptanceTester 48, 49
  FunctionalTester 48, 51
  UnitTester 48, 53
testing
  about 2, 35
  acceptance tests 35, 39
  code coverage 41
  importance 2, 3
  integration tests 35
  integration tests coverage 38
  master test plan 42
  partial view, of application 36, 37
  scope 42
  top-down approach, versus bottom-up
    approach 40
  unit testing coverage 37, 38
  unit tests 35
testing mindset
  obtaining 12, 13
  practical examples 13-15
test quality, improving
  about 155
  acceptance tests' coverage report,
    generating 166-168
  code coverage criteria 156
  code coverage, enabling in
    Codeception 157, 158
  code coverage information, extracting
    for unit tests 158-160
  functional tests, aggregating to unit
    tests 164-166
  unit tests coverage report,
    generating 160-164
tests
  characteristics 12
  passing 87, 88
  passing, global fixtures used 88-90
tests, Codeception
  acceptance tests 48
  functional tests 48
  types 48
  unit tests 48
tests, in Yii 2 60, 61
Tilde operator 25

Twig
  URL 22

U

ubiquitous language 10
unit test
  about 35
  code testing 69
  implementing 67
UnitTester 53
User model
  using 66, 67

V

Vagrant
  about 19
  URL 19
Verify
  about 91, 104
  URL 105
Violations plugin 180

W

WebDriver-led tests
  implementing 138-141
Wildcard 25
working strategy
  defining 33
  user authentication REST interface 35
  user login, from modal window 35

X

XPath 2.0
  about 111
  URL 111
xUnit plugin 180

Y

Yii 2
  about 1
  Codeception, installing 56
  development environment 18
  downloading 17
  environment 18
  features 33, 34
  installing 18
  URL 18
  work flow 19
  working with 30, 31
Yii configuration, for Selenium
  about 137, 138
  browser (required) 138
  host 138
  restart 138
  url (required) 138
  window_size 138
Yii virtual attributes 98-102

Thank you for buying
Learning Yii Testing

About Packt Publishing

Packt, pronounced 'packed', published its first book, *Mastering phpMyAdmin for Effective MySQL Management*, in April 2004, and subsequently continued to specialize in publishing highly focused books on specific technologies and solutions.

Our books and publications share the experiences of your fellow IT professionals in adapting and customizing today's systems, applications, and frameworks. Our solution-based books give you the knowledge and power to customize the software and technologies you're using to get the job done. Packt books are more specific and less general than the IT books you have seen in the past. Our unique business model allows us to bring you more focused information, giving you more of what you need to know, and less of what you don't.

Packt is a modern yet unique publishing company that focuses on producing quality, cutting-edge books for communities of developers, administrators, and newbies alike. For more information, please visit our website at www.packtpub.com.

About Packt Open Source

In 2010, Packt launched two new brands, Packt Open Source and Packt Enterprise, in order to continue its focus on specialization. This book is part of the Packt Open Source brand, home to books published on software built around open source licenses, and offering information to anybody from advanced developers to budding web designers. The Open Source brand also runs Packt's Open Source Royalty Scheme, by which Packt gives a royalty to each open source project about whose software a book is sold.

Writing for Packt

We welcome all inquiries from people who are interested in authoring. Book proposals should be sent to author@packtpub.com. If your book idea is still at an early stage and you would like to discuss it first before writing a formal book proposal, then please contact us; one of our commissioning editors will get in touch with you.

We're not just looking for published authors; if you have strong technical skills but no writing experience, our experienced editors can help you develop a writing career, or simply get some additional reward for your expertise.

open source
community experience distilled

Yii Application Development Cookbook
Second Edition
ISBN: 978-1-78216-310-7   Paperback: 408 pages

A Cookbook covering both practical Yii application development tips and the most important Yii features

1. Learn how to use Yii even more efficiently.

2. Full of practically useful solutions and concepts you can use in your application.

3. Both important Yii concept descriptions and practical recipes are inside.

Web Application Development with Yii and PHP
ISBN: 978-1-84951-872-7   Paperback: 332 pages

Learn the Yii application development framework by taking a step-by-step approach to building a Web-based project task tracking system from conception through production deployment

1. A step-by-step guide to creating a modern Web application using PHP, MySQL, and Yii.

2. Build a real-world, user-based, database-driven project task management application using the Yii development framework.

3. Start with a general idea, and finish with deploying to production, learning everything about Yii in between, from "A"ctive record to "Z"ii component library.

Please check **www.PacktPub.com** for information on our titles

www.ingramcontent.com/pod-product-compliance
Lightning Source LLC
Chambersburg PA
CBHW060554060326
40690CB00017B/3702